BUILDING A MODEL RAILROAD WITH PERSONALITY

MODEL RAILROADING HANDBOOK NO. 18

By John Olson   Photography by the author

Edited by Jim Kelly

The material in this book first appeared as articles in MODEL RAILROADER magazine

First printing, 1983. Second printing, 1985. Third printing, 1987. Fourth printing, 1989. Fifth printing, 1991.

Meet the Jerome & Southwestern: a railroad with personality

Our first look at a railroad we'll see built step by step

PERSONALITY — even a small model railroad can have it, and that's what I went for in planning and building the Jerome & Southwestern, a bite-and-kick HO scale Arizona railroad set in a region where copper was king. I'll be telling you how I built the J&S in the chapters that follow this one, and I aim to make it all as clear as mountain creek water, with lots of step-by-step photos. Although the J&S was built with beginning railroaders especially in mind, I think you old pros will find some interesting ideas and techniques too. Either way, I hope you'll all enjoy reading the J&S story.

The Jerome & Southwestern, like thousands of other small model railroads, measures 4 x 8 feet, the size of a standard sheet of plywood. Remember, I had beginners in mind. I also had these other good reasons for building a 4 x 8:

● A 4 x 8 is pretty much the smallest feasible unit for a "usable" HO standard gauge railroad.

● You can easily dress it up later with free-form meandering table edges.

● The railroad is small enough to be easily portable in one piece.

● Hey, you gotta start somewhere!

You'll find the materials for building the Jerome & Southwestern easy to locate. I used common lumber sizes and readily available hardware, and I stuck with model railroad products likely to be available at the local hobby shop. The track plan is very simple, calling for readily available and inexpensive Atlas switches and flexible track.

The key to building and enjoying a successful pike isn't buying the most expensive products available; it's using what you can afford creatively. In some areas you can't cut corners — stout benchwork and

A slow-moving Jerome & Southwestern freight runs through Jerome Junction and across the high bridge spanning Apache Gorge. The Athearn SW1500 and Model Die Casting boxcab are J&S's most up-to-date engines. Mingus Mountain hovers in the distance.

This photo by Gary Krueger; all others by the author

Highest point on the Jerome & Southwestern is at Furlow's Folly no. 1, a dock serving the Verde Copper King Mine. The Heisler locomotive, of AHM parentage, has just spotted a string of empties in the abandoned entrance and is preparing to pull the loaded cars off the dock for the harrowing trip down the mountain.

John with Firmam E. Wood, SP agent. Heidi Olson photo

Meet John Olson

JOHN is a fellow who needs no introduction to many of our readers. He may be only 34, but he's an old-timer when it comes to model railroading, having been at it for 15 years. A superb photographer as well as modeler, John is especially adept at creating layouts with a western flavor. His modeling is an expression of his lively imagination and is always alive with details, figures, and activity; he attributes many of his ideas to the inspiration he found in the work of John Allen.

John's HO and HOn3 Mescal Lines and HOn3 Cielo Lumber Co. have been featured in MODEL RAILROADER often, including several striking cover photos. His modeling and photos have been featured widely in other American publications and also in Japanese modeling magazines. He also enjoys working with model railroading manufacturers and has done design consultation work for Campbell, HO West, Plastruct, Model Dynamics, Krasel, Kemtron, and Chooch.

John received a bachelor's degree from CSUF, where he was trained to be a marine biologist. He worked for a year for the California Department of Marine Resources, then joined Lion Country Safari as a Ranger of Exotic Animals, a job that involved working in the open with wild animals.

Since 1974 John has been a designer with WED Enterprises, the Disney organization responsible for designing and developing theme park projects. John had a large hand in designing and supervising the construction of the Big Thunder Mountain RR. attractions at both Disneyland in California and Disney World in Florida. He lives in California, but lately has been traveling extensively and doing most of his work in Florida and the new Tokyo Disneyland in Japan. In an interesting turnabout on his hobby activity, one of John's professional specialties is supervising the construction of full-sized simulated rockwork.

John likes to spend his free time poking around in out-of-the-way places, particularly in the hills and deserts of California, Nevada, and Arizona. These experiences all contribute to the abundance of character we find in his modeling efforts.

Jim Kelly

A copper train crosses above the Verde cut-off on its way down to Jerome Junction. Going up or down, the locomotive stays below the train to prevent runaways. The abandoned truck probably hit one rut too many on the McLellan toll road, a treacherous route that comes nearer being a dry wash than a highway.

reliable trackwork are absolutely necessary — but scenery, structures, and rolling stock need not be expensive. A little planning and patience and you can make even the most humble plastic kits come alive — I'll be showing you how.

The J&S was designed to be a railroad that could grow, and it did just that. The Back Alley & Wharf RR. is a 2 x 6-foot extension added after I completed the J&S. The BA&W serves the industrial heart of Grandt's Harbor, a city on a bay, and building this addition allowed me to try a brand of modeling entirely different from what I'd done on the J&S. I'll tell you all about the BA&W in Chapter 9, but you can skip ahead to page 56 if you like.

BLUEPRINT FOR A RAILROAD

Most first railroads aren't planned; they just happen. We start with a loop of track, add a spur, build a mountain at one end — sound familiar? Usually the day comes, though, when we decide to stop everything and start over, this time with a plan, and I don't mean just a track plan, but rather a layout plan based on a theme or concept. A real railroad has a place and a purpose, and we learn to design model railroads that do too. I'm not much on hard and fast rules about this hobby, but I think that's one good one: a model railroad ought to have a theme.

Once you've had some experience at de-

Dos Hermanos is a desert tank town. The heat during the day is blistering, but cool evening breezes power the windmill that pumps the deep well, keeping the tank full. Supplies for the Jerome mines are often trucked here and transferred to railroad cars for the last leg of the trip.

HISTORIC JEROME

INSPIRATION FOR AN HO RAILROAD

Scale in miles
½ 0 ½ 1 1½ 2 2½

MAP AREA
ARIZONA
Phoenix

To Drake

Verde Valley RR.
(Santa Fe)

United Verde & Pacific RR.
(Abandoned narrow gauge)

Verde Tunnel &
Smelter RR.
(Abandoned)

Smelter

To Copper
(Jerome Jct.)

Open pit

Horseshoe Curve

Hopewell
Tunnel

CLARKDALE

COTTONWOOD

Josephine
Tunnel

Arizona Extension RR.
(Abandoned)

JEROME

Alt 89

BLACK HILLS

CLEOPATRA HILL

To Prescott

Clemenceau Smelter

To Sedona

VERDE VALLEY

Verde River

Verde Tunnel & Smelter 0-6-0 no. 2 backs down the hill from
Hopewell with a loaded ore train for the smelter at Clarkdale

James L. Gayner

Here's a list of books about Jerome:
● James W. Brewer, *Jerome* (Globe, Ariz.: Southwest Parks
and Monuments Assoc., 1979)
● David F. Myrick, *Pioneer Arizona Railroads* (Golden: Col-
orado Railroad Museum, 1968) and *Railroads of Arizona,
Vols.I and II* (San Diego: Howell North, 1980)
● Russell Wahmann, *Cleopatra's Railroads* (Jerome, Ariz.:
Jerome Community Service Organization, 1975)
● Herbert V. Young, *Ghosts of Cleopatra Hill* (Jerome,
Ariz.: Jerome Historical Society, 1974) and *They Came to
Jerome* (Jerome Historical Society, 1972)

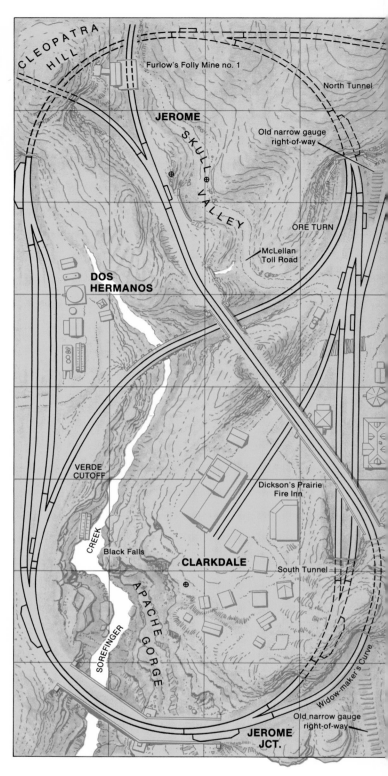

CLEOPATRA HILL

Furlow's Folly Mine no. 1

North Tunnel

JEROME

SKULL VALLEY

Old narrow gauge
right-of-way

ORE TURN

McLellan
Toll Road

DOS
HERMANOS

VERDE
CUTOFF

Dickson's Prairie
Fire Inn

CREEK

Black Falls

CLARKDALE

South Tunnel

SOREFINGER

APACHE GORGE

Widow-maker's Curve

Old narrow gauge
right-of-way

JEROME
JCT.

signing and building model railroads it
gets to be a bit like magic. You envision an
empire, then call it forth as a tangible,
miniature world filled with all the features
and life you imagined — and it all begins
with just a little tickle between the ears!

That tickle came for me when I was driv-
ing through central Arizona in 1979 with
my father, James Olson. We happened
upon Jerome late one afternoon. Here was
an Old West mining town hacked into the
side of a mountain. The road to Jerome is a
pageant of engineering, architectural, and
cultural artifacts proclaiming a time when

the town flourished. Blasted cuts in solid
rock, guard rails made of scrap rail, 30-
year-old vehicles left abandoned — I was
engulfed immediately in the charisma of
the town and told my father right then
what a great model railroad it would make.

Not long after getting home I followed up
on my visit to Jerome with a trip to the li-
brary, a planning step I heartily recommend in planning any model railroad. The
more you know about why and how the
real railroads were built, the more convinc-
ing your model railroad will be — and it'll
have more personality. The local color and

history will give you some interesting and
unusual modeling ideas that you would
never have arrived at on your own.

Every town exists for a reason, and I
found out the reason for Jerome had been
copper. Jerome sits on the side of Cleopatra
Hill, and inside that mountain is an enormous mine with 15 miles of tunnels. The
town is so extensively undermined that the
streets and foundations are buckling and
cracking continually. The mine is closed
now, but over a 70-year period a billion
dollars' worth of copper ore was dug out.

In boom periods Jerome was home to as

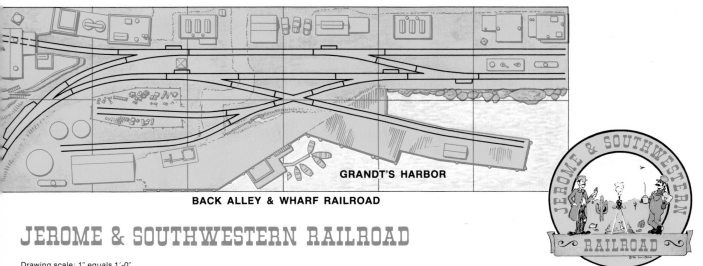

GRANDT'S HARBOR

BACK ALLEY & WHARF RAILROAD

JEROME & SOUTHWESTERN RAILROAD

Drawing scale: 1″ equals 1′-0″

At Clarkdale the ore cars are weighed before delivery to the dock on the Back Alley & Wharf. The Prairie Fire Inn, half hidden behind the bridge, relies heavily on the patronage of Jerome & Southwestern personnel.

The tiny buildings in Clarkdale's "Old Town" section reflect a boomtown heritage. Only a few decades ago undertaker Potts was an extremely busy man and fortunate that Boot Hill was only a few hundred feet away.

many as 20,000 people, including some with colorful names like Boxcar Riley, Elderberry Bill, and Handsome Dan Murphy. Among the notorious ladies were the Cuban Queen, Madame Pearl, and Jennie Banters.

The elevation of Jerome is more or less 5000 feet, depending on where you are—the town is spread out over many hundreds of feet vertically. In summer the temperature routinely goes above 100, and in August comes a monsoon season with afternoon thunderstorms. Winter covers the region with a thin veil of snow. The sunsets seen from Jerome are spectacular as the Mogollon Rim across the Verde Valley is set ablaze with crimson and magenta.

JEROME REVISITED

Eighteen months after my first visit I went back to Jerome looking for more information and inspiration to use in developing my HO scale J&S.

Nowadays you might call Jerome a living ghost town—about 300 people live there. Jerome's modern residents are eager to share its rich history. The Jerome Historical Society in the heart of town has lots of good displays, books, and a helpful, friendly staff. The Douglas Mansion, near the Little Daisy Mine, is now an Arizona state historic park, with many first-class displays, lectures, and models to see and touch. I think you'll find that local histori-

cal groups like these all over the country are extremely useful sources when it comes to researching local railroad activity.

I spent several hours talking to John McMillan, who was especially kind and told me about how Jerome had been 50 years ago. He ought to know. He worked 21 years at the mine — 16 years below the ground, 5 above — then served as a fireman on the Verde Tunnel & Smelter RR. Now he's the on-site manager for Phelps-Dodge properties. John's father, George, was an engineer on the narrow gauge United Verde & Pacific Ry., and survived a rollover in locomotive no. 8.

JEROME'S RAILROADS

Jerome's history is fascinating, and you can learn more about it by reading the books in the list I've included with this installment.

Narrow gauge, standard gauge, electric overhead, and electric battery — Jerome eventually had all of that, but until 1895 the ore rolled out in wagons pulled by horses or mules. Then came the United Verde & Pacific, a 3-foot gauge line that came in like a roller coaster from the west and a connection with the Santa Fe, Prescott & Phoenix. The UV&P ran 26 miles from Jerome Junction (later renamed Copper) to Jerome, going up and down 3 percent grades and through 187 curves, some as sharp as 24 degrees. At Horseshoe Curve the

passengers could look over into the cab of the locomotive that was pulling them. An even bigger thrill came after getting off the train at the depot. The last short leg into town was by horse and buggy down a 45 degree incline called "the slide."

The UV&P served Jerome until 1920, but it was doomed as of 1911 when the Santa Fe built a standard gauge line, the Verde Valley RR., into Clarkdale. This became Jerome's railroad connection with the outside world and remains so today.

In 1912 Jerome's United Verde Copper Co. decided it needed a larger smelter. There was no place to put it on Cleopatra Hill so they built it at Clarkdale, down in the valley. Two thousand feet separate Jerome and Clarkdale vertically — 6 miles as the stone rolls. The company built the Verde Tunnel & Smelter RR. to connect the smelter with Hopewell Tunnel, an entrance to the mine halfway up the mountain, but 1000 feet below Jerome. Completed in 1915, the VT&S soon came to be called the "Very Tired & Sleepy."

In a few more years the VT&S was pushed from Hopewell up to Jerome and came to be 11 miles long, 4 percent up all the way, with sharp curves and four switchbacks. Whether going up or down, the locomotives stayed below the trains to prevent runaways. The VT&S served Jerome until the mine was shut down in 1951.

Another important railroad to the area

other. All of these are quite useful in layout planning because you can use them to make a small pike look bigger by dividing it into a series of scenes.

I didn't try to model specific prototype features on my Jerome & Southwestern, but the railroad is a distillation of my experience in the Jerome area. Jerome gave my railroad its theme — its look, and its feel, and its purpose. The J&S exists to haul the copper ore off Cleopatra Hill and start it on its way to the world.

Imagine a train of two or three loaded ore cars waiting on the rickety dock at Furlow's Folly no. 1, highest point on the railroad. Coming upgrade is a train of three empties, shoved by a hard-chuffing Heisler. (The locomotive always stays on the down side of J&S mine trains to keep from adding to the growing pile of wrecked runaways at Widow-maker's Curve). The Heisler spots the empties in the abandoned tunnel, backs off, and switches onto the mine dock to pick up the loads.

Before leaving, our engine has to pull the empties back out of the tunnel and spot them on the dock for loading. Then *very carefully* he eases back down the mountain, through the short tunnel, and across breathtaking Apache Gorge. He can breathe easier as he settles into the flat run across the desert to dos Hermanos.

Dos Hermanos is a quiet, isolated desert town that exists only to serve the railroad. The town's heritage is Spanish and its name translates to "two brothers." Our train is left on the passing siding here, and after both the crew and engine take on water and fuel they pick up a string of empties for a return trip up the hill.

The J&S's small fleet of diesel switchers handles the trains now, wheeling the ore cars on to Clarkdale, a town that began as an Apache Indian encampment and still has a bit of a wild streak, although it's becoming more refined almost by the day. At Clarkdale the ore cars are weighed at the scale and the figures are carefully entered in the company ledgers. The crews usually take on nourishment at Dickson's Prairie Fire Inn before exercising their running rights on the Back Alley & Wharf and delivering the loaded cars to the pier — the ore is still a boat ride away from the smelter.

While ore traffic is what the J&S is all about, there are other trains. There are through freights that use the J&S as a bridge route and usually get routed through quickly. The lowly peddler freights get stuck in the hole for everything, and some days it seems they spend most of their time just waiting. There's a daily mixed train — usually two or three freight cars and a combination mail-baggage-passenger car — that makes the run from Clarkdale to dos Hermanos every day. The U. S. Mail sack is usually pretty light, but it gives the mixed train priority over all the others, even the "golden" copper trains.

TIME TO GET STARTED

If you don't have the time or space to build a layout right now, I hope you'll come along with me anyway as I tell about the J&S. Sit back in that armchair and dream about the day when you can drive home that first nail in your benchwork. Or, if you do have the time, the space, and the energy, turn the page and meet me in the workshop so we can start building the Jerome & Southwestern.

The ore mined at Jerome is shipped out from the dock on the Back Alley & Wharf RR. Theoretically the mine and the dock are many miles apart, but as you can see here, they are in fact separated by only a few feet. Over on the Jerome & Southwestern part of the layout another ore train is making its way down from the mine. Meanwhile a livestock train is heading for Clarkdale.

was the Arizona Extension RR., a line built to haul ore from the mine to a different smelter, this one at Clemenceau, later called Cottonwood.

These were the above-ground railroads; two others were below. Hopewell Tunnel had a 7200-foot-long underground railroad that was double-tracked, ran off trolley wire, operated 20- to 25-ton locomotives on 250-volt DC current, and used 40-ton drop-bottom ore cars. At the 500-foot level was

another underground railroad. It was three-rail dual gauge, standard and 18″. Men were moved on the standard gauge, materials on the narrow. Battery powered locomotives were used here.

DRAWING ON THE PROTOTYPE

The Jerome area is rich in features perfect for model railroads: tight curves, lots of vertical track separation, and quick transitions from one type of scenery to an-

This photo by Gary Krueger. All others by the author.

Benchwork and roadbed for the Jerome & Southwestern

Time to get out the tools and start building our railroad with personality

IN THE first chapter I introduced the Jerome & Southwestern, an HO layout with lots of scratch-and-kick personality inspired by a copper-mining region in Arizona. Although the 4 x 8-foot J&S is the size of most first model railroads, I tried to capture some of the vastness of western scenery in that 32 square feet, and I hope you'll agree the layout looks larger than it is. That's because it's carefully divided by hills and ridges into scenes to be looked at one by one. Just as important as the hills are the ravines and gorges that extend *below* track level, and in this chapter I'll be showing you how to build a type of benchwork that allows us to model these low-lying features with a minimum of fuss.

Adding the mountains and gorges helped me avoid that round-and-round-the-Christmas tree syndrome, but I also made sure the track wasn't flat and level. Grades and vertical track separation add interest to a layout and make the running distances seem

longer. Using the cookie-cutter construction I'll be describing, building these features really isn't hard at all.

I used the time-honored, butt-joint framework system because it's easy to build and strong. When combined with the plywood roadbed it allows as much flexibility in locating track as we are likely to require. For a complete discussion of benchwork of all types refer to Linn Westcott's HOW TO BUILD MODEL RAILROAD BENCHWORK, published by Kalmbach Books.

BENCHWORK MEANT TO LAST

Look at the photos of my benchwork and you'll see I built it solid. I have friends who've accused me of over-nailing, over-clamping, and using enough white glue to drown a horse standing on a ladder. Maybe they're right, but I'm a real believer in doing things right the first time. I've seen too many teary-eyed model railroaders whose benchwork had sagged and warped, twist-

ing and ruining the track. All they could do was start over, losing some beautiful scenery and detailing in the bargain.

I wanted my benchwork to be strong enough to stand up to extreme temperature and humidity changes. Well and good, you say, but you'll have no such problems. You aim to have an air-conditioned room with even temperature control. Fine, but what about when you're adding plaster and paint? We torture the benchwork quite a bit just in the course of completing a model railroad.

I had some other good reasons for building the Jerome & Southwestern's benchwork as strong and rigid as I could. After all, this is possibly your first railroad — I hope it is — and I wanted it to be fully portable, easy to modify as your interests develop further, and free-standing without depending on walls or other outside supports. With these qualities the J&S could become the nucleus for expansion to a larger layout in the future.

It's hard to believe that this photo was taken on a 4 x 8-foot model railroad. Vertical elements divide the J&S into scenes and make it look larger. The mine spur ridge divides the layout diagonally.

It'll take you only a few days to build the benchwork for the J&S, and in a way it's too bad it goes so quickly. Speaking for myself, I thoroughly enjoy building benchwork. I've spent weeks, even months, hunched over a drawing board designing the layout. Once the mental "wars" with myself are over, I enjoy the good physical exercise of banging nails and raising a little three-dimensional havoc. A short work session is quickly rewarded with the first tangible evidence of the empire to come.

MATERIALS

The bill of materials lists exactly what I used. Let's look here at my reasons for choosing these materials.

● **Pine.** Here's a wood soft enough to accept nails easily, yet plenty strong for our needs. I used it for all the framing except the contour boards. I also used it for the corner blocks, risers, and cleats. The topnotch, clear-grade stuff I used was prob-

ably overkill, but I got a good supply at great prices. Grade 2 pine with tight, solid knots as few and small as possible is fine in most cases.

Pick through all the lumber and select only well-seasoned, straight-grained boards. Green lumber will likely warp and shrink during the first few months after you've built the benchwork, causing a world of troubles with roadbed and track alignment.

● **Fir.** This wood is too hard and splits too easily to be used as benchwork framing, but I used common 2 x 4 fir studs for legs.

● **Plywood.** Strength and flexibility make plywood an ideal choice for your subroadbed. This is no place to skimp on quality with a cheap construction grade of lumber. I also used ½"-plywood for scenery contours, control panel shelves, and some diagonal bracing for the legs.

● **Masonite.** Handsome control panels and backdrop boards are easy to make with this material. The sawdust is very irritat-

ing so use a dust mask when sawing or sanding Masonite.

● **Homasote.** This is a pressed paper product I used for roadbed. It deadens sound and accepts and holds spikes and track nails well. It's also fairly resistant to changes in humidity, especially when it's laminated to ½" plywood subroadbed. Homasote is often difficult to locate, but if you get out the Yellow Pages and start calling lumberyards you'll probably be successful. Avoid Celotex and other coarse, loosely pressed paper and fiber products.

● **Oak veneer plywood.** This is optional. I used it to build the storage and magazine cabinets. I also used 12 board feet of oak for facing and molding.

TOOLS

Here's a list of the tools I used to build my benchwork. You probably already have most of them in your shop.

● Pencils and marking pens.
● Framing hammer. (That's a regular carpenter's hammer, folks.)
● Combination or carpenter's square.
● Tape measure.
● Drill and bits.
● Saber saw. You'll need some coarse blades for pine and some fine blades for plywood and Homasote.
● Clamps. Bar clamps are best; C clamps will do very nicely.
● Table saw. If you don't have access to a table saw, cut-off saw, or at least a hand-held circular saw, I recommend you have a lumberyard cut the benchwork components. Clean, square board ends are important for strong joints.

BUILDING THE GRID

Before you start building, check your lists to make sure you have gathered all the tools, lumber, and supplies in one place. You don't want to get caught short at some crisis point and have to go running off to a store that probably isn't open anyway.

I assembled the J&S benchwork upside down on the floor because the top is in one flat plane, unlike the bottom where the gorge contour boards create an uneven surface.

This is a good time to have a buddy help you, as the benchwork is awkward and flimsy during early assembly. Work on a clean, flat area like a garage or basement floor. As you go along brace the work against a wall or some other immovable object so your hammer blows don't loosen joints made earlier.

Many modelers will insist that benchwork should be assembled with screws, but that's too time-consuming and costly to

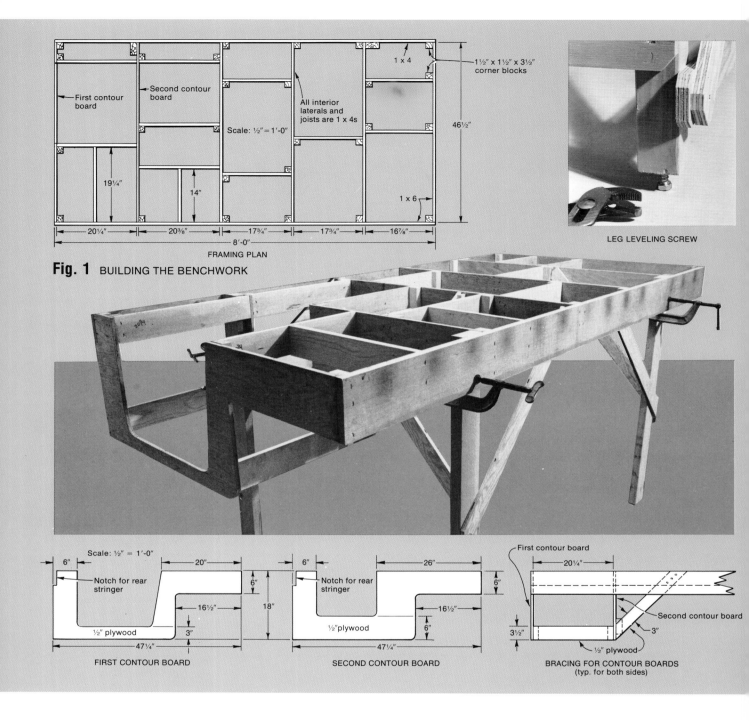

Fig. 1 BUILDING THE BENCHWORK

FRAMING PLAN

First contour board

Second contour board

All interior laterals and joists are 1 x 4s

Scale: ½" = 1'-0"

1 x 4

1½" x 1½" x 3½" corner blocks

46½"

1 x 6

19¼"

14"

20¼"   20⅜"   17¾"   17¾"   16⅞"

8'-0"

LEG LEVELING SCREW

Scale: ½" = 1'-0"

6"   20"   6"   26"   First contour board   20¼"

Notch for rear stringer

6"

18"

16½"

½" plywood   3"

47¼"

FIRST CONTOUR BOARD

Notch for rear stringer

6"

16½"

½" plywood   6"

47¼"

SECOND CONTOUR BOARD

Second contour board

3½"   3"

½" plywood

BRACING FOR CONTOUR BOARDS
(typ. for both sides)

suit me. Glue, clamps, and nails will do just fine. Should the roadbed need to be relocated, I simply cut the riser, elevate it to the new position, and glue a splice board over the cut.

I started at the gorge end of the layout and worked toward the other end. This procedure allowed me to seat all the interior joists and laterals securely against the last piece installed.

Here are the steps for assembling the J&S benchwork.

● Cut all the pieces to size and label them. See fig. 1.

● Mark the two side rails where the laterals will join them.

● Nail the side rails to the first plywood gorge contour board.

● Place the second gorge contour board between the stringers and glue and nail it

in place, using the 20¼"-long interior joists as spacers.

● Glue and nail the 20¼" joists in place.

● Continue installing laterals and joists until you're finished. Wipe any excess glue from the joints with a damp rag as you go.

● Add corner blocks, not just to the four outside corners, but one to each joint. You needn't nail them. Extra hammering on the frame before the glue sets isn't good practice, so simply glue and clamp each block.

These blocks contributed significantly to the benchwork's rigidity. Later, once the plywood subroadbed was added, it became impossible to twist the grid out of square.

● Let the frame dry overnight. By the next morning you're ready to add the legs and get this project off the ground.

● Clamp the legs temporarily in place.

You'll find this easy to do because you built the frame upside down.

● Add sway braces to the legs, using 1"-long no. 8 flathead screws.

● Turn the benchwork right side up and bolt the legs permanently. Adjust the screws in the leg ends to level the benchwork.

I built my benchwork on rather tall legs so I could store toolboxes, sawhorses, and other supplies underneath and out of the way. Later I cut them shorter so they could team with the storage cabinets in supporting the finished railroad. Eventually the front of the railroad was supported by cabinets, the rear by the legs.

LAYING OUT THE FULL-SIZE TRACK PLAN

Now we're ready to draw the full-size paper pattern we'll use for cutting the ply-

Fig. 2

LAYING OUT THE FULL-SIZE TRACK PLAN

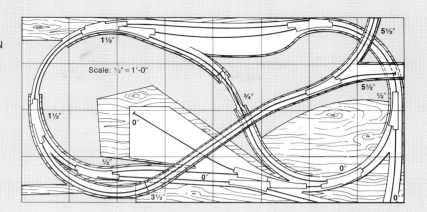

Materials for benchwork

No.	Material	Size	Use
1	½" plywood	4 x 8 feet	Subroadbed
2	½" plywood	2 x 4 feet	Contour boards, sway braces
1	½" Homasote	4 x 8 feet	Roadbed
1	1 x 6 pine	8 feet	Front stringer
1	1 x 4 pine	8 feet	Rear stringer
4	1" x 4" pine*	46½"	Laterals
3	1" x 4" pine*	20⅜"	Joists
2	1" x 4" pine*	20¼"	Joists
3	1" x 4" pine*	17¼"	Joists
2	1" x 4" pine*	16⅞"	Joists
1	1" x 4" pine*	18"	Lateral joist
1	1" x 4" pine*	14"	Lateral joist
34	1½" x 1½" pine	3½"	Corner blocks
2	1½" x 1½" pine	6"	Corner blocks
4	2 x 4 fir	44½"	Legs

* The breakdown into lengths is for convenience in cutting. If you're cutting your own 1x4s to length, you'll need 42 feet of material (including the rear stringer).

1	pint white glue	
1	lb. no. 8 box nails	
8	⅜"-dia. x 3" bolts with 8 nuts and 16 washers	
24	1"-long no. 8 flathead screws	

John works on a full-size paper track plan taped to the wall

Track used for the J&S

Atlas
    Custom-Line Supreme*
        Curved right-hand, 2
        Curved left-hand, 3
    Custom-Line
        No. 4, left-hand, 2
        No. 4, right-hand, 4
    Curvable track, 3
* See story for remarks on availability

Draw mine spur on
tracing paper overlay

A yardstick makes
a handy trammel

wood and the Homasote. See fig. 2. If you're building the J&S just as I did, then you're working from my finished plan and won't have the problems that come with initial planning. If you want to make some changes, though, or build a railroad of your own design, then you'll be interested in how I solved some of the late-stage design problems.

A few words of warning: Atlas has discontinued their Custom-Line Supreme brand of turnouts, so the curved turnouts I used may be hard to find or unavailable. Atlas plans to offer curved turnouts of the same configuration in their Custom-Line Mark II series, but not for a very long time. In the meantime, don't despair. Both Tyco and Shinohara offer curved turnouts that you can substitute easily.

We won't be laying track until the next chapter, but I'm including the list of track requirements in fig. 2, so you can shop for track at the same time you pick up your lumber and other benchwork materials.

Blowing up an original scale track plan to full size is fun, but it can be quite frustrating if you take the scale drawing too literally. Only after the track plan has been laid out full scale can you really see if the turnouts, crossings, and grades will fit.

I thought my scale drawing of the J&S was fine, but it turned out I had to flip-flop several of the turnouts. That's why I suggest that if you're designing your own layout you hold off on buying *all* the turnouts until you know exactly what you need.

I did my full-size planning with some templates I made on a copying machine, placing real turnouts upside-down on the glass and making six copies of each basic

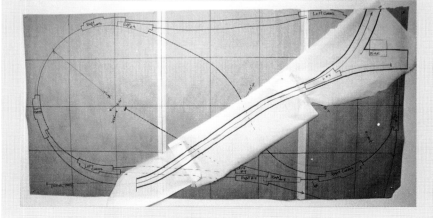

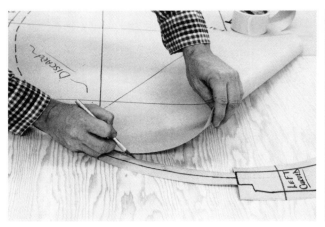 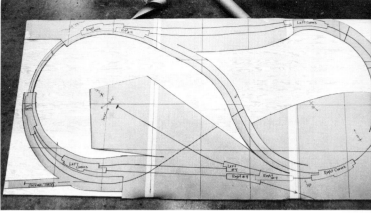

◄ Fig. 3. Left to far right. After taping his paper plan to the plywood, John trimmed out the discard areas with an X-acto knife. He transferred his cutting lines to the wood with a felt-tip pen, then started sawing.

◄ Fig. 4. Left to right. Marking turnout locations on the Homasote was tricky. First John outlined the roadbed. Then he cut the paper and marked the track center lines. Last he cut out and outlined the turnout template.

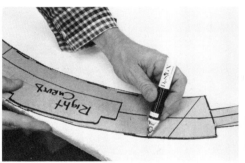  

◄ Fig. 5. Four photos above. John nailed the 0″ elevation plywood to the benchwork, then clamped on risers to establish grades. After adjustments he marked the risers for cutting and added cleats. He glued and nailed the subroadbed to the risers, then glued on and clamped the Homasote.

type: no. 4 right-hand, no. 4 left-hand, right-hand curved, and left-hand curved. I rubber-cemented the copies to 1/16"-thick cardboard and then cut them out.

Here are the steps for making the large drawing:

• Tape enough brown Kraft paper together to make a 4 x 8-foot piece.

• Tape the paper to the wall. Drawing against the wall enabled me to back up several feet and check for fluidity and smoothness of track lines.

• Draw a 1-foot grid pattern on the paper.

• Make a trammel for drawing curves. I made mine from a yardstick by drilling 1/8" holes along the center line at inch marks 16 through 36.

• Lay out the long curves at each end of the layout. These define the placement of all the rest of your track.

• Pin your turnout templates in place and draw in the connecting tracks. If you're building my track plan exactly, you know what track components you're using and can trace around the actual turnouts.

• Be prepared to readjust some turnout locations. Adjustments are easy to make with an eraser now, but they'd be a bear once the track was laid. I moved some of my turnouts several times until I found the most pleasing lines.

• Avoid regularity. As space allowed I increased the radius of some of the curves towards their ends, giving me pseudo-transition curves. A lurch from straight track to 18"-radius curve can be disconcerting. Also,

I avoided constant-radius curves wherever I could. They tend to make a layout look toylike.

• Once you're satisfied with your track center lines, darken them with a black felt-tip pen and outline the turnouts.

• Mark the discard areas that will be cut away.

• Measure 1½" from each side of the center lines and mark the subroadbed edges. Then draw in the "cookie cutter" cut lines.

MARKING AND CUTTING THE PLYWOOD AND HOMASOTE

Now you're ready to transfer the pattern to your 4 x 8-foot sheet of ½" plywood. See fig. 3. Cut the discard sections out of the paper pattern, then mark these areas on the plywood. Mark each of the subroadbed and "cookie cutter" cut lines.

Figure 4 shows how to mark the Homasote roadbed. Use pushpins to pin the paper plan to the 4 x 8-foot sheet of ½" Homasote. Accurately trace the roadbed lines ¼" inside the subroadbed lines (The roadbed will be ½" narrower than the subroadbed.)

Use a hobby knife to cut a bit at a time along the track center lines, drawing the lines onto the Homasote with a felt-tip marker as you go. As you get to each turnout, outline it and note the type used. This process will destroy the by-now flimsy paperdoll-like plan, so check your work often.

Supporting your work on sawhorses, cut out the subroadbed and roadbed with a saber saw. Handle these shapes carefully as they are easy to break at this stage.

BUILDING THE RIGHT-OF-WAY

Now we're ready to fasten the subroadbed to the benchwork.

• Position the plywood subroadbed on the benchwork. Refer to the track plan in fig. 2 and mark the elevations.

• Nail the 0" elevation areas temporarily to the benchwork, as shown in fig. 5.

• Clamp 12"-long, untrimmed risers to the benchwork so the subroadbed is elevated to the desired heights.

• Take your time. Study the entire layout to see that the vertical transitions are smooth and the elevated horizontal areas are indeed level. Make sure the grades are steep enough to clear lower tracks at crossovers yet not so steep as to look bad or hinder train operation.

• Saw your "cookie cutter" separation lines further if necessary to ease vertical transitions. Note how the one-piece plywood subroadbed flows smoothly from level to level because of the natural springing action of the wood.

Once you've made all the fine adjustments and are happy with the results, you're ready to start fastening the subroadbed in place permanently.

• Mark those areas of benchwork that will support plywood directly at the 0" elevation. Lift the plywood, apply white glue to the top edges of the benchwork pieces, and replace the plywood — double-checking for good alignment at the corners. Nail the 0" elevation sections to the benchwork.

• Now make your permanent risers. See

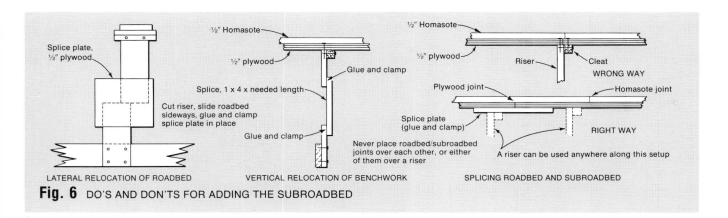

Splice plate, ½" plywood

½" Homasote

½" plywood

Cut riser, slide roadbed sideways, glue and clamp splice plate in place

LATERAL RELOCATION OF ROADBED

½" Homasote

½" plywood

Glue and clamp

Splice, 1 x 4 x needed length

Glue and clamp

Never place roadbed/subroadbed joints over each other, or either of them over a riser

VERTICAL RELOCATION OF BENCHWORK

½" Homasote

½" plywood

Riser

Cleat

WRONG WAY

Plywood joint

Homasote joint

Splice plate (glue and clamp)

RIGHT WAY

A riser can be used anywhere along this setup

SPLICING ROADBED AND SUBROADBED

Fig. 6 DO'S AND DON'TS FOR ADDING THE SUBROADBED

Fig. 7. The Apache Gorge Bridge, kitbashed from plastic bridges, eventually went here. The plywood provided enough strength to lay track and start running trains.

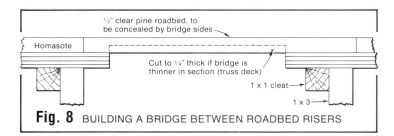

½" clear pine roadbed, to be concealed by bridge sides →

Homasote

Cut to ¼" thick if bridge is thinner in section (truss deck)

1 x 1 cleat

1 x 3

Fig. 8 BUILDING A BRIDGE BETWEEN ROADBED RISERS

Fig. 9. Top to bottom. John built the pile deck bridge in the center of the layout early so he wouldn't damage scenery and structures doing it later. First he cut the chunky stabilizing brace from a length of 2 x 4, then glued and clamped it to the roadbed. After the glue had set, he cut away the roadbed and installed a ½" pine deck, thinning the visible portion to ¼". Using ¼" dowels and stripwood he made the 1¾"-high bents at the workbench, then cemented them to the deck.

fig. 5. Mark the riser's length and mark where it intersects the joist. Glue and nail a cleat to the top. Hold the riser in position and check to see if the top should be beveled for subroadbed on a grade.

• Apply white glue to the mating surfaces where the riser contacts the benchwork and the subroadbed. Clamp the riser to the benchwork and nail it in place. Nail the subroadbed to the top of the riser. The glue should set in 2 hours.

• Continue adding risers until no span of more than 16" remains. Sometimes you must be clever in designing and locating your risers to solve unique access problems. The railroad is now tremendously strong and rigid, yet not too heavy.

ADDING THE HOMASOTE ROADBED

Adding the Homasote to the plywood subroadbed is an easy job and so it proceeds quickly. See fig. 6 for some do's and don'ts.

The Homasote is quite absorbent, so spread the white glue on the subroadbed generously. Immediately clamp and nail the roadbed. The Homasote is soft so don't hammer too hard and create dimples that could cause track problems later.

Wherever possible I used firm boards to clamp the roadbed in a sandwich, the idea being to distribute the pressure evenly and avoid distortion. This technique also helps where two pieces of roadbed butt together

and you want to avoid a step forming between the two pieces.

Once the glue has dried and you've removed the clamps, fill any gaps between the roadbed butt joints. Dap brand spackling compound works well for this.

You don't have to build all the bridges to get the trains rolling. As fig. 7 shows, you can leave the subroadbed and roadbed where a bridge eventually will go and lay the track right over it. Later you can cut out the roadbed and install a bridge. Figure 8 shows the technique involved.

I thought it would be best at least to get the preliminary work done on those bridges in the middle of the layout. Figures 9 and 10 show what I did.

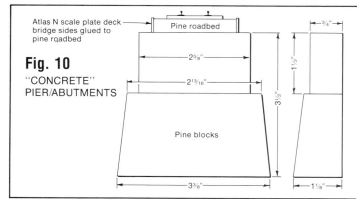

Atlas N scale plate deck bridge sides glued to pine roadbed

Pine roadbed

¾"

Fig. 10

"CONCRETE" PIER/ABUTMENTS

2⅜"

2¹³/₁₆"

1½"

3½"

Pine blocks

3⅜"

1⅛"

CABINETRY

I designed the Jerome & Southwestern to go in a family recreation room, and I felt it more than worth the effort to make some nice-looking cabinets and storage shelves to fit under and along the front edge of the railroad. See fig. 11.

I designed the four oak storage cabinets as 3-foot-wide by 3-foot-high modules so they could be used individually or in combinations elsewhere in the house, should their job of holding up the J&S come to an end.

The car and locomotive storage shelf is particularly handy. I use my shelf to display convention cars I've collected at NMRA-sponsored meets.

ADIOS

We're off to a good, solid start. Next time better wear your gandy-dancer togs. Now that the grading crews are finished, we'll be laying track. It won't be long until those mules that bring the copper down from Jerome are replaced by iron horses.

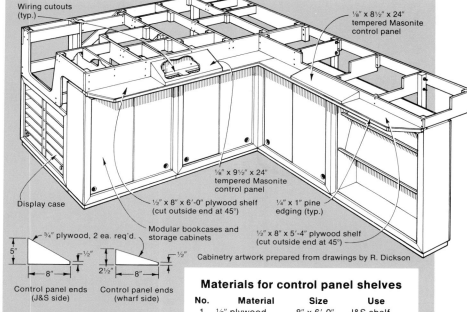

Wiring cutouts (typ.)

⅛" x 8½" x 24" tempered Masonite control panel

Display case

½" x 8" x 6'-0" plywood shelf (cut outside end at 45°)

⅛" x 9½" x 24" tempered Masonite control panel

¼" x 1" pine edging (typ.)

Modular bookcases and storage cabinets

½" x 8" x 5'-4" plywood shelf (cut outside end at 45°)

Cabinetry artwork prepared from drawings by R. Dickson

¾" plywood, 2 ea. req'd.

Control panel ends (J&S side)

Control panel ends (wharf side)

CONTROL PANEL SHELVES

4' x 8' x ¾" plywood, 2 ea. req'd.

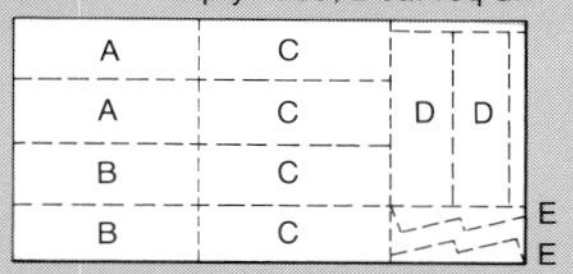

CUTTING PATTERN

A = Top, 12" x 34½"   B = Bottom, 12" x 34½"
C = Side, 12" x 36"   D = Shelf, 11" x 34½"
E = Magazine support

Materials for control panel shelves

No.	Material	Size	Use
1	½" plywood	8" x 6'-0"	J&S shelf
1	½" plywood	8" x 5'-0"	BA&W shelf*
1	¼" pine	1" x 12'-0"	Facing
1	⅛" Masonite	9½" x 24"	J&S panel
1	⅛" Masonite	8½" x 24"	BA&W panel*
2	¾" plywood	5" x 8"	Slope blocks
2	¾" plywood	2½" x 8	Slope blocks
2	Piano hinges	¾" x 20"	Hinges
24	Small finish nails		
	Glue and paint		

*The Back Alley & Wharf extension will come last in this series, but it's most convenient to specify the cabinetry materials for it now.

Materials for 4 bookcase/storage units

Two 4 x 8-foot pieces of ¾" oak veneer plywood to be cut to the following sizes:

8	12" x 36"	Sides
8	12" x 34½"	Tops & bottoms
4	11" x 34¼"	Shelves
3	See drawing	Magazine rack

One 12-foot length of 1" x 12" oak board cut to the following sizes:

16	1⅞" x 36"	Molding (45-degree end cuts)
8	¼" x 34½"	Magazine rack rails

Two 4 x 8-foot pieces of ¼" plywood cut to the following sizes:

4	35½" x 35½"	Back panels

One 4 x 8-foot piece of ⅛" Masonite cut to the following sizes: (leftovers can be used for control panels)

6	18" x 33¾" for doors (save leftovers for control panels)	
20	shelf pegs for ¼" holes	
6	aluminum door tracks, 34" (plus screws)	
1	white glue, 1 pint	
1	Watco walnut finishing oil, 1 quart	
1	lb. 1½" finishing nails	
16	Teflon or carpet covered tacks for feet	

BOOKCASE/STORAGE UNITS

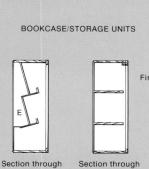

Section through magazine rack

Section through bookcase/storage

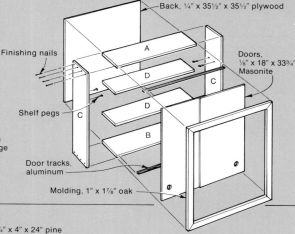

Back, ¼" x 35½" x 35½" plywood

Finishing nails

Doors, ⅛" x 18" x 33¾" Masonite

Shelf pegs

Door tracks, aluminum

Molding, 1" x 1⅞" oak

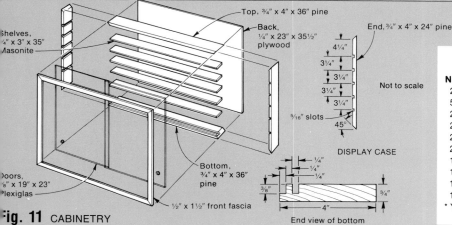

Shelves, ¼" x 3" x 35" Masonite

Top, ¾" x 4" x 36" pine

Back, ¼" x 23" x 35½" plywood

End, ¾" x 4" x 24" pine

4¼"
3¼"
3¼"
3¼"
3¼"

Not to scale

5/16" slots

45°

Doors, ⅛" x 19" x 23" Plexiglas

Bottom, ¾" x 4" x 36" pine

½" x 1½" front fascia

DISPLAY CASE

¼"
¼"
¼"
3/8"
¾"
4"

End view of bottom

Materials for display case

No.	Material	Size	Use
2	⅛" Plexiglas	19" x 23"	Sliding doors
5	¼" Masonite	3" x 34½"	Shelves
2	¾" x 4" pine*	24"	Ends
2	¾" x 4" pine*	36"	Top and bottom
2	½" x 1½" pine*	24"	Facing
2	½" x 1½" pine*	36"	Facing
1	¼" Masonite	23½" x 35½"	Back
1	box small finishing nails		
1	white glue, 1 pint		
1	quart paint or stain		

* You could substitute oak to match modular units

Fig. 11 CABINETRY

JEROME & SOUTHWESTERN
3
RAILROAD

Track and control for the Jerome & Southwestern

We get the trains rolling on the railroad with personality

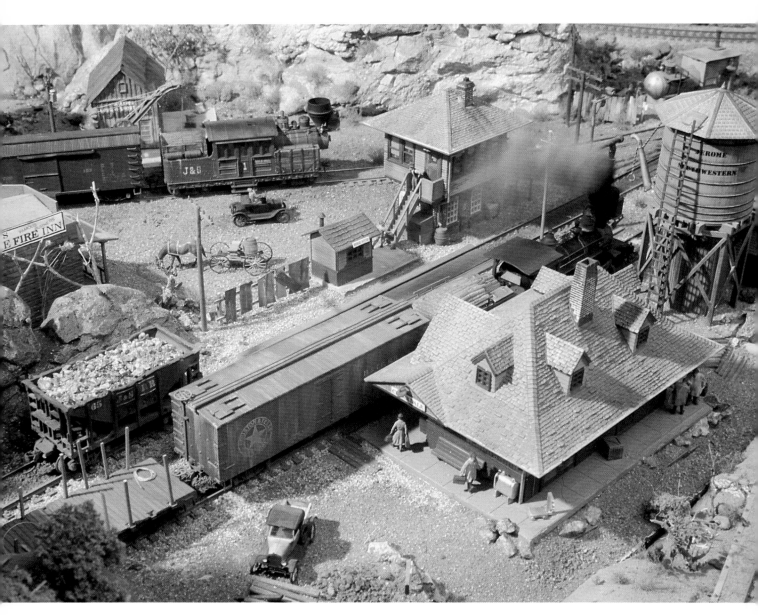

Wiring a model railroad is like building the underwater portion of an iceberg, so here's a photo to keep us inspired. Students of the modern J&S will notice something missing in this vintage photo. The long bridge over Clarkdale hadn't been built yet.

IN Chapter 2 we built sturdy benchwork and roadbed for the Jerome & Southwestern, being careful to arrange things so some rugged western scenery would fit right in later on. Now the railroad with personality is ready to come alive. We'll lay track and switches, hook up some wires, and then stand back as that diesel engine turns over a few times, then coughs, catches, and slowly comes up to operating speed. As that first locomotive inches forward on its first run, imagination will start filling in the sights, sounds, and smells — our pile of lumber will have become a full-fledged railroad with a character all its own.

First, though, we'll need to negotiate with some foundries and sawmills back east and get those flatcars loaded with rails, ties, and spikes moving in our direction. Take a look at the bill of materials and you'll see my track supplies came out of New Jersey — I used Atlas switches and flexible track throughout. These are easy

to work with and reliable, but as I mentioned last time, you could run into a problem. Atlas is no longer making the curved turnouts, and you may have trouble locating any. Not to worry, though. Both Tyco and Shinohara make curved turnouts you can substitute.

LAYING TRACK

The track plan shows where the pieces go. With no further ado, let's roll out the work train and start laying track. Here's how to do it, step by step:

● Carefully look over the turnouts as you take them from their packages. The National Model Railroad Association (NMRA) makes a standards gauge for HO track. You should be able to find one at your hobby shop. It's wise to invest in one and use it frequently to check clearances.

Look carefully to see there's no plastic flash along the inside rail surfaces. This can be quite thin and difficult to see, yet if it rises high enough, it can throw trains off

the track. If you find some, trim it away with a hobby knife.

Make sure the throwbar and points move freely. Atlas turnouts have stamped point rails. As fig. 1 shows, these sometimes require bending with needle-nose pliers so that the tops of the point rails will close tightly against the stock rails. If the points are blunt, file them sharp. Otherwise the wheel flanges can pick the point, that is, bump up and over the point rather than

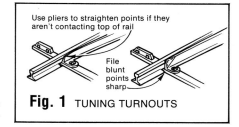

Use pliers to straighten points if they aren't contacting top of rail

File blunt points sharp

Fig. 1 TUNING TURNOUTS

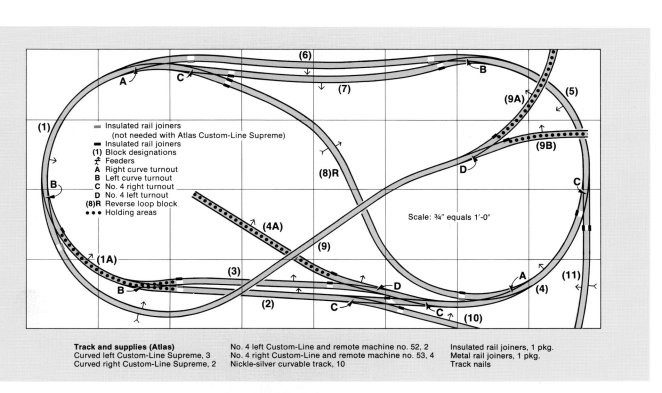

Scale: ¾" equals 1'-0"

Legend:
- Insulated rail joiners (not needed with Atlas Custom-Line Supreme)
- Insulated rail joiners
- **(1)** Block designations
- Feeders
- **A** Right curve turnout
- **B** Left curve turnout
- **C** No. 4 right turnout
- **D** No. 4 left turnout
- **(8)R** Reverse loop block
- ••• Holding areas

Track and supplies (Atlas)

Curved left Custom-Line Supreme, 3	No. 4 left Custom-Line and remote machine no. 52, 2	Insulated rail joiners, 1 pkg.
Curved right Custom-Line Supreme, 2	No. 4 right Custom-Line and remote machine no. 53, 4	Metal rail joiners, 1 pkg.
	Nickle-silver curvable track, 10	Track nails

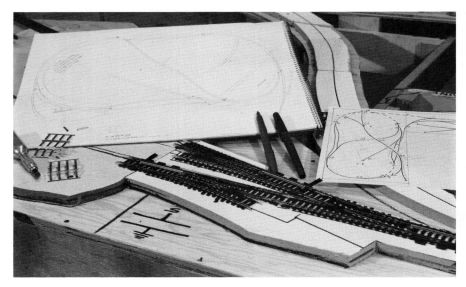

Fig. 2. Turnout placement doesn't lend itself to fine adjustments, so the first step in laying track was laying turnout combinations. The track plan indicates where John used insulating joiners.

Fig. 3. John removed the plastic webbing between ties in some turnouts so he could slightly curve the rails to achieve smoother track flow.

guide along it following the desired route.

● Assemble turnout combinations for yard areas first, as shown in fig. 2. In some places you'll be joining the rails with metal joiners; in other places you'll be using plastic. The track plan shows you which type to use where. The plastic joiners establish the electrically isolated blocks necessary for our control system — more about that later.

Using track nails, lightly tack these turnout combinations in place over the track center lines and turnout outlines drawn on the Homasote.

● Work your way around the railroad and tack the remaining turnouts in place. Now look over your work to see that the center lines between turnouts flow gracefully with no cramping.

You can modify a turnout slightly if the routes don't diverge from it quite the way you want. As shown in fig. 3, cut slots in the "between-the-ties" plastic web on the underside and gently flex the track to the curvature you want.

● Start filling in between turnouts with flexible track, using the techniques shown in fig. 4. I know three methods for cutting rail:

You can use a razor saw, but this is the slowest method and also the most difficult.

The rail and plastic ties must be held firmly or the saw's teeth will grab the rail and yank it out of the ties.

Using rail nippers is the easiest way, but then you have to file the cut-off ends so the rail joiners will slip on easily — of course, some filing may be necessary with any of the methods.

Given my druthers I prefer a motor tool equipped with an abrasive cut-off disc. I can't think of a good argument for why it's best — I just like it best. If I have any doubt about the lengths I cut the rails long and then trim them to fit.

Rails lengthen ever so slightly with increases in temperature, and this expansion can cause kinking if the rail ends are butted tightly together; therefore, I leave gaps between rail ends, trying for about $\frac{1}{64}$". I like to use a good-rolling truck and a freight car to test rail joints for smoothness as I go.

Some modelers solder rail joints to ensure electrical conductivity. I don't, because then allowance for expansion and contraction can't be made. Rather, I run an electrical feeder wire to each and every section of rail to ensure electrical continuity — more on that later. I'll solder a rail joint only for mechanical reasons, say in

order to get a smooth joint within a curve.

● Once you've tacked down all the main-line track, check and adjust it as necessary. Your eyes are the best instrument for checking your track for smooth flow. Sight along the rail, using the reflected shine of a distant light on the railhead as a guide. Sudden breaks in the shine can signal trouble spots. Check for kinks, and too-quick entry into curves.

● Loosen the track nails and adjust the track as necessary. When all is well, drive the nails down, using a nail set as shown in fig. 5. Stop just before the nail heads touch the tie tops. You want to leave the ties a little "breathing room" and not distort them. You can make final adjustments by tapping the nail heads to one side or the other with your nail set.

● The holes already in the track are useful, but you'll probably need some more, placed where they can do you the most good. As fig. 6 shows, you can add more holes with a no. 55 drill held in a pin vise. You want a track nail every 4 or 5 inches, as well as within a tie or two of the last tie in a section.

● Install the sidings and spur tracks, using the same check-as-you-go procedure.

● Use ties from short scraps of flextrack

Fig. 4. Left to right. To lay flexible track John first connected a section at one end. Then he curved it into position and marked it for cutting, laying it

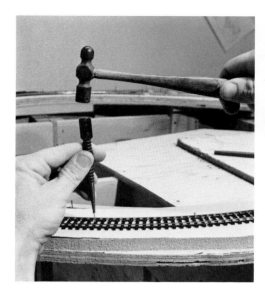

Fig. 5. Once satisfied with the track alignment, John drove the nails down, using a nail set and being careful not to drive the heads tight against the ties.

Fig. 6. The pre-cast holes in plastic ties don't always fall where they're needed. John drilled some extras with a pin vise.

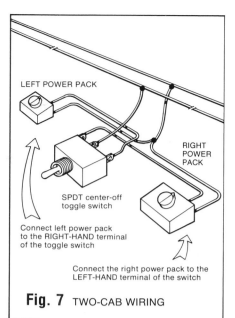

Fig. 7 TWO-CAB WIRING

LEFT POWER PACK

RIGHT POWER PACK

SPDT center-off toggle switch

Connect left power pack to the RIGHT-HAND terminal of the toggle switch

Connect the right power pack to the LEFT-HAND terminal of the switch

to replace the ties removed for rail joiner clearance. Carve the plastic spikes away with a hobby knife and be sure the ties slide under the rail joiner without lifting the rail and causing a hump.

I tried something new for me with the J&S, just to see how well it could handle temperature changes. I took the railroad outside on a warm sunny day (not in direct sunlight, however) and allowed everything to warm up, expand, or do whatever it might. I looked over all the rail joints and sighted along the straight tracks — all appeared okay.

Then I took the railroad back indoors, where it was some 40 degrees cooler, and watched for changes. The rail gaps opened and closed a bit, but no buckling occurred. Seems to me, then, you won't have rail kinking problems with the J&S — provided you didn't build the benchwork out of green lumber which could shrink. After all, house temperatures seldom vary by 40 degrees. Maybe you'd get such extremes in garages and attics, but I've never had problems with my Mescal Lines narrow gauge

railroad. It's built quite similarly and is located in our garage where it's 40 degrees in the winter and 100 degrees in the summer.

TWO-CAB CONTROL

Now, if we can just get some electricity into the tracks and from there into the engines, we'll be in business. I wired the J&S with a system called two-cab wiring. It's been around a long time and is hard to beat for small railroads. The system's biggest advantage is it allows at least two engineers to operate their trains independently and simultaneously anywhere on the layout, as long as their locomotives don't get into the same electrical block. The system is easy to install, operate, and troubleshoot, should a gremlin creep in later.

Figure 7 illustrates the basic principle of the system. Each zone, or block as it is commonly called, has one rail that is wired directly to the power pack. A feeder wire from the other rail leads to a single-pole, double-throw (SPDT) toggle switch with a

center-off position. The power to the track comes from power pack (or cab) A when the toggle is thrown left and from power pack B when the toggle is throw right. The block receives no power when the toggle is in the center-off position.

As the track plan shows, I divided the J&S into eleven electrically isolated blocks. The track plan is represented on the control panel by a schematic diagram. See fig. 8. I mounted the toggles right on the schematic, so it's easy to find the toggle that controls a particular section of track — even for the first-time operator.

Operating a train with this system is simple. As your engine approaches the next block you flip the toggle for that block toward the power pack you're using. As you leave a block, you return the toggle for that block to the center-off position. You continue throwing toggles in this leapfrog fashion as your train progresses around the layout.

If only one engineer is going to run only one locomotive, simply flip all the toggles towards the power pack to be used and op-

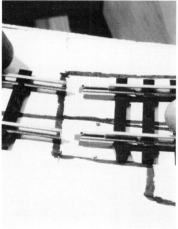

right on the turnout it would join. He then cut the rail, removed some ties to provide joiner clearance, and connected the track pieces. Voila! a perfect job.

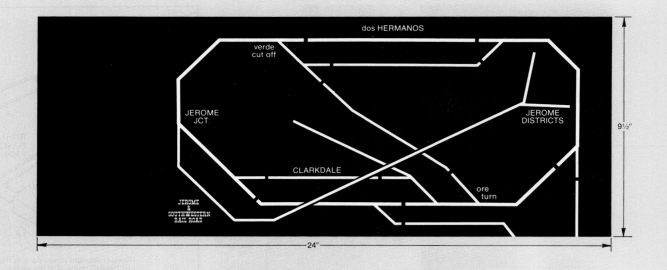

Fig. 8 CONTROL PANEL
Scale: ¼" = 1"

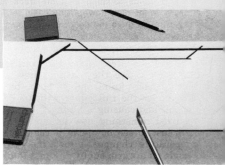

erate as though the railroad were all one big electrical block.

THE REST OF THE SYSTEM

Figure 9 is a wiring diagram for everything electrical on the railroad. My two stationary power packs are a Troller Momentum 2.5 and an MRC Control Master II. Just for fun I added a walkaround controller that can be used in place of one of the standard packs.

A walkaround unit, as the name implies, allows you to follow along as your train rocks and sways over the right-of-way and strains on the grades. You're right there with the crew, heart in your throat, as trestles squeak and complain at your passing.

You can buy good walkaround throttles; I made mine, following the instructions in Peter Thorne's book, PRACTICAL ELECTRONICS PROJECTS FOR MODEL RAILROADERS, published by Kalmbach Publishing Co. A DPDT (double pole, double throw) toggle mounted on the control panel allows me to switch from stationary power pack to walkaround and vice versa quickly.

Also mounted on the control panel are the push buttons that control my electric switch machines. I need only push the button corresponding to the route I want to take and the turnout will snap into alignment.

Included in my control system is a booster unit for the switch machine power supply. This is a capacitor-discharge machine that stores a large amount of energy which can be delivered to the switch machines almost instantaneously, causing the points to snap firmly. Tri-Delt, Circuitron, and B-L Hobby Products all offer these devices, or you can build your own. Thorne's electronics book, mentioned above, will show you how.

BUILDING THE CONTROL PANEL

Most of the wires we'll connect to the tracks and the switch machines run directly to the control panel, so the job will go easier if we make the panel before wiring the layout.

I cut my 9½" x 24" panel from ⅛"-thick tempered Masonite. This size is plenty large enough to accommodate the toggles, push buttons, and meters without being cluttered. You could easily make your panel smaller, as miniature toggle switches and push buttons are available, but you would run the risk of crowding the controls and making it difficult for the operators to read the track diagram.

I wanted my control panel to be brown with yellow lines so it would come near matching the official J&S corporate colors: Tuscan Red and Denver & Rio Grande Western Yellow. Voila! The control panel would be in character with the model railroad — it would add to its personality.

Step one was to paint the Masonite with Krylon Pastel Yellow, using a spray can. Yellow covers poorly, so I applied several light coats, then allowed the panel to dry overnight.

Next I laid out the track plan schematic on the yellow surface, using a soft lead pencil. See fig. 10. I used more than proportionate spacing between sidings so pudgy fingers would be able to reach all the block control toggles easily.

Using the penciled lines as a guide, I laid on Chartpak graphic tape to mask off the track lines, using ¼" tape for the main line and ⅛" for the secondary routes and spurs. I did the longest lines first and the shortest last, making sure that all tape joints overlapped. I cut ⅛"-wide gaps in the tape to represent the block boundaries. Using a metal ruler, I·pressed the tape snugly against the panel so the coat of

brown spray paint would not seep under.

I sprayed on Krylon Dark Brown in several light coats, let it dry for 24 hours, then peeled off the graphic tape and erased the penciled guide lines. I used Prestype brand dry transfers to label the towns and major sidings, then I sprayed the panel with a protective coat of Krylon clear finish.

After another 24-hour drying period I drilled holes for the toggles, push buttons, and panel lights. To prevent chipping I was careful to use a sharp drill, and I placed a block of wood behind the Masonite before drilling. With this done, I installed the toggle switches, push buttons, and lights.

You could hinge the panel, but I simply glued small pine blocks at each underside corner and let gravity do the rest. I want the backs of my panels as accessible as possible to make repairs, modifications, and additions easy.

TWO MORE WIRING PRINCIPLES

Now we're ready to start wiring. I used common return wiring, a method that saves about 40 percent on the amount of wire needed. With this method we establish our electrical blocks by using insulating joiners in only one rail. The other rail, the common-return rail, is not gapped.

Look at the track plan and you'll see that the outside rail is the common return. The only insulating joiners in it were put there to isolate reversing segments. The insulated joiners dividing the layout into control blocks are all located on the inside rail.

We have one last wiring principle to look at. Notice that any train taking the cut-off that runs diagonally across the middle of

J&S electrical supplies

Quantity	Item	Purpose
10	SPDT toggles, center off	Blocks 1-11
3	SPST toggles	On/off blocks 1, 4, and 9
5	DPDT toggles, center off	Reverse block 8 and cab reversing switches
2	12-V panel lights, green	Reverse block polarity indicators
22	Push buttons (11 red, 11 green), normally open	Turnouts
60 feet	No. 12 copper wire	Common return
300 feet	No. 20 copper wire	Feeder wires
2	Power packs, your choice*	

*If neither of your packs has an ammeter, you may want to add a 0- to 2-amp full-scale meter to your panel.

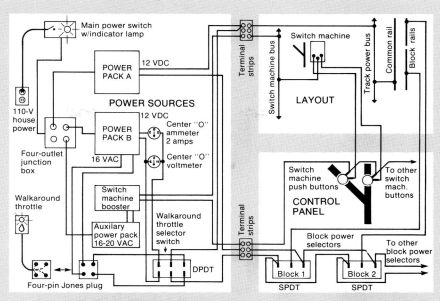

Fig. 9 OVERALL POWER SCHEMATIC

Fig. 10 CONTROL PANEL PAINTING PROCEDURE

Left to right. To make the Masonite control panel John first spray-painted it yellow, then added lines with a soft lead pencil. After masking the lines with chart tape, he sprayed the panel brown. Pulling away the tape left a professional-looking brown panel with yellow lines.

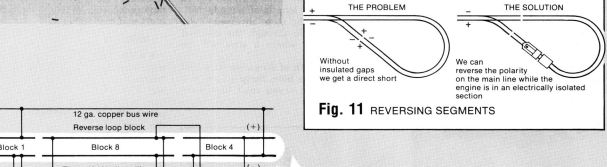

THE PROBLEM — THE SOLUTION

Without insulated gaps we get a direct short

We can reverse the polarity on the main line while the engine is in an electrically isolated section

Fig. 11 REVERSING SEGMENTS

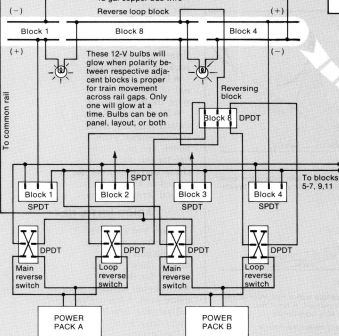

12 ga. copper bus wire
Reverse loop block

These 12-V bulbs will glow when polarity between respective adjacent blocks is proper for train movement across rail gaps. Only one will glow at a time. Bulbs can be on panel, layout, or both.

Reversing block

To blocks 5-7, 9,11

Fig. 12 REVERSE BLOCK WIRING

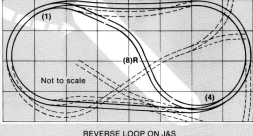

REVERSE LOOP ON J&S

OPERATION:

As train approaches reverse loop, set loop direction switch so that green lamp at entrance end glows. Once the locomotive has fully entered loop, reverse the main direction switch so that the green lamp at exit end of reverse loop now glows. Train can now leave loop

23

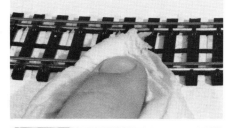

← Fig. 13. Top to bottom. To attach a feeder wire John first drills a hole in the roadbed and pokes the wire through. After stripping about 1″ of insulation he bends the wire to the shape shown. He adds a drop of flux, using a toothpick, then touches the soldering iron to the joint, removing it quickly once the solder flows. John recommends keeping a small bubble of solder on the hot tip. Because the solder is premelted, the job will take less time, thus reducing the chance of damaging plastic ties. A damp cloth applied to the joint cools it quickly. John cleans away excess solder with a file and follows up with a Bright Boy track cleaner. When the track is painted the feeder wire will virtually disappear.

the layout will end up reversing its direction of travel. This gives us flexible operation, but also introduces an electrical problem. Figure 11 shows what would happen if we laid this track without making some sort of special provision. We'd have a short circuit.

To eliminate the short circuit we could add insulated joiners, as shown in fig. 11 also. This would work fine until we tried to run an engine across the gap. As soon as the engine entered, it would receive current of reversed polarity and go backwards, only to be driven immediately forward again. Usually in this situation a locomotive will shuttle back and forth violently until something breaks and it finds peace.

We solve the problem by introducing a reversing segment electrically isolated from the rest of the track. While the engine is in this segment, we can throw a switch that reverses the polarity on the main line and sets it up to receive the engine.

On the control panel I used a 12-volt light at each end of the block to indicate polarity for approaching trains. Figure 12 shows how they are wired. If the light is on at the end of the block the train is approaching, the polarity of the reversing segment is right for receiving it.

ONE STEP AT A TIME

So much for theory. Let's plug in the soldering iron and go to work! Here are the steps in wiring the layout:

• Remember, I don't recommend soldering rail joints, so we'll need a feeder wire connected to each length of outside rail. Figure 13 shows the steps involved. First we drill a 1/16″ hole through the roadbed alongside the rail where a wire will be soldered.

• Cut a 16″ length of 20 gauge wire and poke it through the hole. Strip off an inch or so of insulation — you can't beat wire

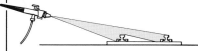

A
Paint track from all angles with base colors such as Floquil Roof Brown, Grimy Black, or Weathered Black

B
Spray from a low angle with a rust color so that only rail sides are painted. A good rust color is 60% Floquil Rust, 40% Roof Brown

After 1-2 days drying time, clean railheads with a Bright Boy

Fig. 14 PAINTING TRACK

strippers for stripping insulation! Clean the side of the rail with emery paper or a file, and solder on the feeder.

• Record all your connections on a master plan. You'll be amazed at how hard feeders are to find once you've painted the track!

• We'll connect all these feeder wires to a bus wire that makes a loop under the layout and is connected to one of the variable DC terminals on each power pack. Drill ½″ holes in the joists near the perimeter of the layout and thread this 12 gauge common-return wire through them.

• Now crawl about under the benchwork (or turn the railroad on its side if you want to make the job easy) and solder the feeder wires to the common return wire. I like to connect 4 or 5 wires at one place on the bus wire, to save on stripping and soldering.

• Now for the inside, gapped rails. Solder feeder wires to all the rails in each block, gang them together, and label them as per the wiring diagram. You will have eleven labeled bunches of wire.

• Now, taking them one block at a time, connect wires to the corresponding toggles on your control panel. Consult the wiring diagram and connect the toggles to the second terminals on your power packs. Put a locomotive on the proper track and see if it runs. Once the wire checks out, solder it and move on to the next one.

• Proceed one block at a time until you have finished. Checking each connection as you go may be time-consuming, but it'll help you locate problems easily. It sure beats wiring a layout without testing, then having to disconnect the wires one by one until you solve a problem.

WIRING THE SWITCH MACHINES

• We'll also use a bus wire for the common terminals on the switch machines. Number 12 wire will also do in this case, and we can string it through the same holes we used for the common-return track power wire. Connect this bus wire to one of the terminals on your 16-volt AC power source. You could use the AC terminals on your power pack, but I recommend against it. Trains would slow down every time you threw a turnout. A separate small power pack or transformer is better.

• Determine which is the common terminal of each switch machine and connect a wire from it to the common-return wire.

• Run wires from the two remaining switch machine terminals, connecting them to the proper push buttons on the control panel. The buttons have two terminals each, one for the wire coming from the switch machine and the other for a wire to be connected to a second bus wire that runs to the second terminal on your power source.

ADIOS UNTIL NEXT TIME

Once you've wired the layout and the trains are running with complete reliability, you can paint the track, using the techniques shown in fig. 14. You'll be amazed at how far this takes you down the road toward scenic realism, which is where we're going next. After we've added scenery we'll ballast the track and stain it here and there with some fuel oil and soot.

I'm getting ahead of myself, though. Time for us both to take some time off to just relax and run the trains. Next time we'll build some mountains.

Operating the J&S is even more fun if an operator can be close to his train as he puts it through its paces. John built the hand-held walkaround controller shown here following instructions in Peter J. Thorne's book, PRACTICAL ELECTRONIC PROJECTS FOR MODEL RAILROADERS. It's an easy-to-build project that adds a lot to the enjoyment of running trains on the J&S.

Terrain for the Jerome & Southwestern

We add hardshell and rock castings to the railroad with personality

YOU'LL love making scenery. In fact, you can't help but love it — there are no critical dimensions, no whiz-kid electrical diagrams, nothing to go wrong — just plain, messy ol' fun! There's nothing mystical about building scenery, either, and you don't have to be an artist. All in all, like most of the other aspects of building the J&S, making the scenery is simply a matter of proceeding from one easy step to the next.

I'll go back and explain each in detail, but here are the basic steps: In this installment we'll shape the land with cardboard strips and add a plaster hardshell. We'll add plaster rocks cast in homemade rubber molds. In the next scenery installment we'll color the rocks with universal dyes and acrylic paints. For real-looking dirt we'll actually use the real thing. Many of our plants will come directly from nature too.

To model any kind of scenery you need to get three elements clearly in mind: form, texture, and color. Let nature be your guide. Study the area you're modeling firsthand whenever the opportunity arises. Take lots of photos and look at them often for reference. Looking again and again at my photos of the Jerome, Ariz., area helped me tremendously in establishing basic shapes, colors, and general principles.

SHAPING THE TERRAIN

To form the major scenic contours I stapled cardboard strips to the benchwork and to each other basket-fashion. This is a method that's been around a long time — John Allen described using it to build his Mt. Alexander in the December 1949 issue of MR — but it's still one of the best techniques, especially for beginners. It's clean and inexpensive. Best of all, you'll find it easy to control and alter the shapes so that you can get just what you want.

Figure 1 shows the steps in making the scenic forms. I began by arming myself with 40 or so 24"-long, 1"-wide cardboard strips; scissors; white glue; a staple gun; and a desk stapler.

It's amazing how quickly the process goes and how rapidly the imagination will fill in terrain once there are a few strips of cardboard in place to suggest the surfaces. If you don't like a particular contour, just bend one strip here and another one there, snip a section out of a strip and staple it back together, add more strips — in general, just keep working until you're satisfied. Figure 2 shows the sort of form you'll end up with.

If there are places where you want more support, you can install plywood formers. Figure 3 shows how I used a ½" plywood contour former along the back edge of the layout. I clamped the board in place temporarily then sketched the profile I wanted. Also note how I've sketched the base of the hill onto the flat tabletop in front of my left hand. This line will be a guide for placing the cardboard strips.

ADDING HARDSHELL

Now that our scenery has a skeleton, it needs skin over the top of it. For that we'll use hardshell, made by dipping paper towels in a thin solution of Hydrocal, an especially hard and strong plaster marketed by U. S. Gypsum.

As fig. 4 shows, make sure you cover your tracks with masking tape before starting to hardshell. Also make sure you protect your floor with plenty of old newspapers! This is a messy operation — sloppy Hydrocal will fall between the cardboard strips, splash on the floor, and fly in all directions!

Figure 5 shows the steps in making hardshell. Run about 2" of tap water into a 2 or 3 gallon rubber bowl and add Hydrocal, mixing all the while with a spatula, until you have a thin batter.

Industrial-grade paper towels, like those used for washing windshields in gas stations, work best. Dip the towels into the Hydrocal so that both sides are fully coated. Place the towels on the cardboard forms so they touch as many strips as possible. Be careful when handling the dipped towels that you keep them from folding up on themselves. They are hard to unfold without losing the Hydrocal coat.

The plaster tends to settle quickly, so stir it frequently. Hydrocal has a working time of 15 to 20 minutes, time enough to cover 4 square feet with two layers.

Place the towels so they overlap each other by half widths, making for a double thickness. Complete both coats on one area at the same time for proper bonding.

Once started, you might as well do the whole railroad. The job took me about 3 hours. The clean-up for two or more sessions would take more time than the work itself.

Figure 6 shows how to use a cheap 1"-paintbrush to jab the towel edges down against the roadbed for good contact. Use the brush to squeegee excess Hydrocal away from the track. The brush is also useful for blending and joining adjacent towels. Swish the brush frequently in a bucket of water to keep it in working order.

Take your time and don't try to work too long with a single batch of plaster. Once the plaster hardens, it literally becomes hard as a rock and you'll find it practically impossible to remove from places where you don't want it.

Use a staple gun to securely and carefully fasten the towels wherever they contact the benchwork and roadbed. Do this before the plaster sets. This will prevent the plaster scenic shell from popping loose later. Staple every 2" to 3" and follow

◀ Even the most veteran engineer finds his heart beating faster when a J&S train swings out over Apache Gorge. It's sure no place for a derailment! ◆ A J&S 0-4-0 backs a supply train down from Jerome. Author Olson casts his plaster rocks in rubber molds and colors them with universal dyes and acrylic paints.

Fig. 1. Left to right. John shapes his terrain with cardboard. First he dabs on white glue and staples a strip. Then he trims the strip and fastens the other end.

up by wiping the slop from the benchwork with a damp cloth. Rinse the Hydrocal thoroughly from the gun and then apply WD-40 or some other spray lubricant to prevent rust and jamming.

RUBBER-MOLD MAKING

Our Southwestern prototype requires rock outcroppings and weather-hewn mountain faces. For these I used plaster castings made in my own latex molds.

Making latex rubber molds of real rocks first developed in the museum diorama in-

dustry years ago and has since become standard practice for many model railroaders. Recently the process has been developed full scale. In my work on the theme park projects at Disneyland and Disney World we have used molds as large as 4 x 8-feet. We cast life-size rocks just as we would miniature rocks on a model railroad, except that we use concrete instead of plaster so our rock castings will stand up to the weather.

You can buy your rock molds at the hobby shop, but it's easy to make them yourself. I've made many in the field,

working on rock faces that were far too large to attempt to take home. Rock mold expeditions make fun family outings. Besides, you'll ensure that your molds are like no one else's — unless they happen to discover the exact same rock you did, and that's highly unlikely!

You are sure to draw inquisitive looks from passers-by while making rock molds in the field. I enjoy making up stories to tell these folks and I don't like to tell the same one twice!

If you can find suitable rocks small

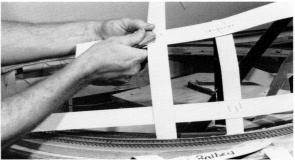

Fig. 2. Left and above. One strip established an old roadbed. Strips stapled to the anchor strips completed the basic form.

Fig. 3. John made a plywood scenery former for the rear of the layout, cutting the cross-hatched area away for access to the inside of the mountain.

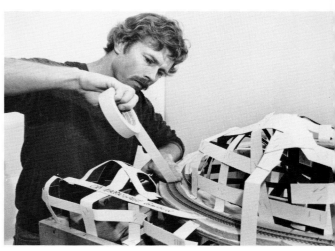

Fig. 4. Here's an important step indeed. John laid down masking tape to protect the rails before he even thought about mixing any plaster.

Scenery tools list

Tool	Use
Staple gun and staples	Fastening cardboard strips
Desk model stapler	Fastening cardboard strips
Spatula	Mixing Hydrocal and plaster
Large rubber tub (3-gal. cap.)	Mixing Hydrocal for hardshell
Small rubber tub (1-qt. cap.)	Mixing plaster for rock molds
Garden pail (1-gal. cap.)	Water supply
Spray bottles	Wetting hardshell
1″ cheap bristle brushes	Working plaster

Scenery materials

Quantity	Item	Use
75	1″-wide x 24″-long cardboard strips	Mountain contours
200	Paper towels (gas station type)	Hardshell
30 lbs.	Hydrocal (U. S. Gypsum A11 or B11)	Hardshell
60 lbs.	Casting plaster (Flintkote Red Tag or other)	Rock castings

enough to carry, take them home with you where working is more convenient. You can put the rocks in your garden once the molds are made and they make great conversation pieces. Just be sure you're not stealing private or government-protected property.

Figure 7 shows how to make rubber rock molds. You'll need the rock of your choice, a quart of liquid rubber latex, several cheap 1″ paintbrushes, a pair of scissors, a few square feet of gauze, and a warm day. Most hobby shops carry a brand or two of

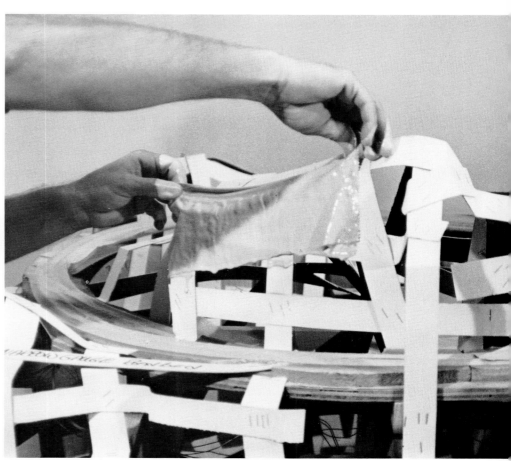

◄ Fig. 5. Top to bottom. To make soupy Hydrocal for hardshell, John adds plaster to the water slowly, stirring frequently. Next he dips a paper towel in the plaster mix. Above. He lays the towel across the cardboard latticework, contacting as many strips as possible for maximum strength.

Fig. 6. Using a cheap brush John tamps the hardshell in alongside the roadbed. Right. He staples the wet hardshell so it won't pop away later.

the latex, but if yours doesn't, check the local craft shop or an art supply store.

Begin by splashing a little water on the rock and then clean it up with one of your brushes. Then paint on the first coat of rubber, working it into the cracks and fissures to pick up all the detail. Allow this coat to air dry completely — approximately 20 minutes at 70 degrees F.

The rubber will change color when it's dry. Mine is a cream color, and when cured it's a darker coffee-with-cream color. Some rubbers are pinkish and turn ruby red.

Apply a second coat evenly and again allow it to completely dry. Rinse your brushes in water after each use.

Cut your gauze into enough 4″ squares to cover the back of the mold twice. Brush on the third coat of latex and immediately work in one layer of gauze. Add another coat of latex, work in the second layer of gauze, and cover it with more latex. The gauze reinforces the mold, making it less likely to tear.

Add another layer or two of latex. You want a mold thick enough to hold wet plaster without collapsing, yet flexible enough to conform to layout landform shapes. With practice you'll learn the thickness that

works best for you. Allow the mold to cure overnight.

Next day peel the mold from the rock and trim the edges with your scissors to make a neat mold.

CASTING ROCKS

It's almost eerie using these latex molds. Such a simple process as mix, pour, apply, and peel yields so wonderful and natural an effect. Let's try working some magic with these molds on the J&S landscape; then you do the same on your pike.

The first thing you'll need is a supply of seasoned water. This will make the plaster set more quickly, saving you a lot of working time. To make seasoned water add a few ounces of raw plaster to the stock water and let it react for 15 to 20 minutes.

While the seasoned water is brewing, you can be getting your other tools and materials together. You'll need 10 to 20 pounds of casting plaster, a rubber spatula, 1-quart-capacity rubber (or other flexible) tubs, your latex molds, and newspapers spread on the floor.

Figure 8 shows how a mold is readied for action. Mix only enough plaster to fill a single mold. Begin with 5 to 6 ounces of

seasoned water in a rubber tub and pour in enough plaster to make a solution the consistency of pancake batter. Quickly pour the smoothly mixed plaster about ½″ deep into a latex mold.

Allow the plaster to set 1 or 2 minutes. You want it hard enough that it won't run out of the mold when you hold it vertically, yet flexible enough that it'll conform to the contours of your hardshell. I check my plaster from time to time by flexing the mold. As soon as small cracks and wrinkles appear, it's ready to be pressed against the hardshell. Should the plaster get a little too dry, simply splash or spray it with water and a good bond between it and the Hydrocal will be ensured.

Figure 9 shows how a casting is applied to the layout. Make sure to wet the hardshell just prior to application. Dry hardshell can pull the water out of a casting so it won't set properly.

Press the mold firmly enough that a little plaster mushes out at the edges; then hold the mold in place until the plaster sets enough that the mold can't spring away, spoiling its contents. Once the plaster has set, move on to the next mold.

The most time-consuming and unpleasant

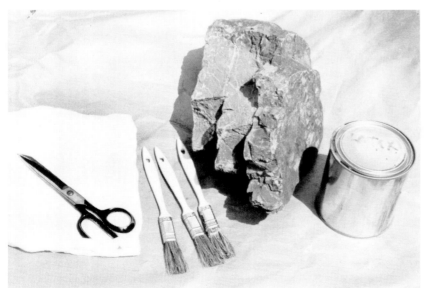  

Fig. 7. To make a rubber rock mold John gathers up gauze, scissors, liquid rubber, brushes, and a rock with fetching qualities. Right. Top to bottom. He works the first coat of rubber into all the nooks and crannies. Several rubber layers later he adds gauze strips to reinforce the mold.

Fig. 8. John pours thin plaster, made with seasoned water, into the mold. Right. In a few minutes the plaster stiffens enough that it won't run out of the mold and can be applied to the hardshell.

Fig. 9. Heidi Olson wets down a portion of the layout in preparation for a rock casting. Above. She must hold the mold in place for 3 or 4 minutes until the plaster sets and will stay put.

Fig. 10. Once the plaster has set hard, the mold is stripped away. Right. Using a hobby knife, John carves away plaster that oozed from under the mold edges, and blends the castings together.

Fig. 11. Hard, rocky soil can be simulated effectively by stippling wet plaster with a stiff brush. Right. John falls back on one of the oldest tricks in the book, carving in erosion lines with a knife.

part of the job is holding the plaster-filled mold against the hardshell. Here are some tricks I use to speed up this operation:

● Involve family, friends, or curious on-lookers by having them hold the freshly filled molds against the hardshell. Usually 3 to 5 minutes is required with each mold.

● Use your molds sequentially so you are filling one, applying another, and peeling the last. Work it like a bucket brigade and you won't have to wait for the complete cycle on any particular mold.

● The most important trick is the seasoned water. Without it you would have to hold the molds in place for as long as 15 minutes. Peel the molds away once the plaster has set enough that it won't crumble as the molds are removed. See fig. 10. The more rugged the rock face, the harder the plaster will have to be to survive the mold removal.

Trim or break away the mushed edge and feather or blend the rockwork into the surrounding terrain. If you are applying a series of adjoining rocks, wait until you've installed them all before blending, but if your rock casting merges with adjacent soil, then smooth up the edge right away.

ADDING SOIL

I know two easy ways to add soil:

● Use real dirt and gravel held in place with glue. This should be done after the hardshell and rocks are painted, so I'll cover it in the next installment.

● Simulate soil with plaster and paint it at the same time you paint the rock castings.

To do this brush a soupy coat of casting plaster over the hardshell, blending up to the previously applied rock castings. As show in fig. 11, stipple the plaster vigorously so a rough, gritty texture appears. Rinse your brush frequently in clean water.

After the plaster sets a bit more, rub here and there with your hand to smooth out some of the rougher areas. Use a random motion.

Figure 11 shows an old trick that still works great, making erosion rivulets by carving the still damp plaster with an X-acto knife. Take your time and the results will be very good.

You can do all the plasterwork on the J&S in a week of spare time or one weekend. As soon as possible pull the masking tape away from the track and clean the rails with a Bright Boy. The tape's adhesive can be difficult to remove if it adheres and hardens. Also, with time the plaster only gets harder, so any trimming and clearance problems are best handled as soon as possible.

Use your NMRA standards gauge to be sure all your track clears the rockwork sufficiently; then run a train over the route to be doubly sure. What a train ride the J&S is now! Two weeks ago this world was all plywood and Homasote, now our train rolls through arroyos, over gorges, and across the vast desert expanses with bravado and newfound purpose.

ADIOS

Stop with the J&S now and you'll have a winter wonderland. When we get together next time we'll stain and paint the rocks and add soil and gravel. There's a surprising amount of plant life in the desert, and we'll be adding that too. See you then.

Right: Author Olson uses warm, reddish colors in foreground areas. The J&S's western theme is established instantly by those big Saguaro cactuses, made from balsa. Far right: This high-stepping woodburner was the J&S's first locomotive and remained a familiar sight on the line until the 1950s. The scenery colors here are the muted browns and yellows that John uses in background areas.

Color comes to the Jerome & Southwestern

We stain the rocks and add soil and plant life to the railroad with personality

FIRST off in this work session we'll add color to the white terrain and rocks we made last time. Before getting out the brushes, spray bottles, and tinting colors, though, let's take a look at the ideas behind the colors we're going to use and some of the fancy special effects we'll achieve with them. With a little trickery we can use color to make the layout look a lot larger than it actually is — more real estate for our money! The Jerome & Southwestern measures only 4 x 8 feet, but it looks larger when you're standing next to it, and bigger yet when you view it in photos.

Achieving the look of long distances took some planning. I designed the J&S to be approached and viewed most often from the Jerome Jct. corner, so I treated that as the foreground. The opposite corner, the Jerome Mining District, I treated as the background. We all know that the way we see objects in the real world is affected by distance. Figure 1 illustrates some differences between the ways objects appear close at hand and at a distance. We can make these differences work for us in designing and building a layout.

If we were building a museum diorama we'd have almost total control over how the viewer would see our modeling, and we could do a great deal to achieve the illusion of distance. We could force the perspective by using N scale buildings and tiny trees in the background. We could lightly overspray everything in the background with blue to suggest haze.

The Jerome & Southwestern is not a museum diorama, however; it's a working model railroad, and the viewer does have considerable freedom to move around it and study it from various positions. We can't go too far in forcing the perspective, otherwise once a person went to the wrong end and looked back, everything would appear ridiculous, much like looking through binoculars from the wrong end. Also, a scale train running through the background would dwarf its surroundings.

Still, if we exercise some common sense, we can use colors to create a sense of distance when the layout is seen from the prime viewing angle, without causing it to look ridiculous when seen from elsewhere. Largely it's a matter of using more vivid colors up front, more subdued ones to the rear.

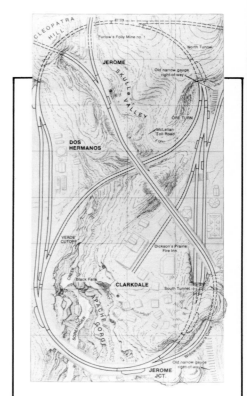

Scenery materials

Tints (universal dyes)

Black	Yellow ochre
Burnt umber	Ultramarine blue
Raw umber	Yellow-orange
Burnt sienna	Gold
Raw sienna	

Artist's acrylics (tubes)
Red oxide
White
Raw umber

Scenery tools
10-12 20-32 ounce containers for mixing dyes
2 spray bottles
1" brush
White glue
Squeeze bottle (for glue)

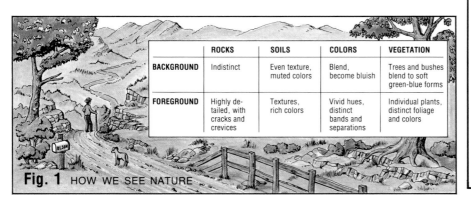

Fig. 1 HOW WE SEE NATURE

	ROCKS	SOILS	COLORS	VEGETATION
BACKGROUND	Indistinct	Even texture, muted colors	Blend, become bluish	Trees and bushes blend to soft green-blue forms
FOREGROUND	Highly detailed, with cracks and crevices	Textures, rich colors	Vivid hues, distinct bands and separations	Individual plants, distinct foliage and colors

◆ Fig. 2. Here's John's equipment laid out for a rock-coloring session. With water as the solvent, there's no odor, no fire hazard. A few drops of universal dye go far in mixing the color washes. The idea is to stain the rocks, not paint them.

◆ Fig. 3. Left to right: To color his foreground rocks and soil, John quickly brushes on quite thin washes, working from light colors towards darker. After applying the colors he sprays on dilute burnt umber with one sprayer and washes it down into the crooks and crannies with water from another. To finish he brushes some acrylic paint on the dominant faces, washing it lightly with spray water; then he brushes on highlights.

◆ Fig. 4. Putting his brush away, John colored his background areas with spray bottles, using light yellows, browns, and grays. A blue overspray imparted the look of landscape seen through haze.

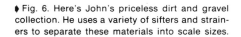

◆ Fig. 5. Risking life and limb our author scrambles up a steep embankment near Jerome, Ariz. There he gathered soil later used on the J&S.

◆ Fig. 6. Here's John's priceless dirt and gravel collection. He uses a variety of sifters and strainers to separate these materials into scale sizes.

Fig. 7. Top to bottom: A Styrofoam cup is handy for applying real dirt and gravel. Using a soft brush, John gently maneuvers the soil and rocks around until he's happy with their positions. The first step in gluing the materials down is soaking them with water from a spray bottle. Then John sprays on diluted white glue. Extra white glue dribbled along the center line with a squeeze bottle fastens the track securely. Once the glue sets, John uses rail nippers to clip off the heads of the track nails, making for improved track appearance.

Fig. 8. Top: There's nothing like the prototype to inspire effective scenery. Jerome, Ariz., sits halfway up Cleopatra Hill. Grasses, shrubs, and trees collect in arroyos and on north-facing mountain slopes where water is slightly more available. Above: Even the flat lowlands are shrouded in vegetation — more than half the ground surface area is covered.

◆ Fig. 9. These specimens are from John's dried weed collection. The clumps shown across the bottom yield sprigs that represent small plants. On the left are yarrow blossoms. Individual buds make good small cactuses. In the middle are juniper leaves. Small sprigs of this are good for cholla cactus. The rosebush roots on the right effectively represent deadwood. With ground foam glued on they can be Palo Verde plants. Flock or ground foam can change the color and textures of these and many other dried plants.

◆ Fig. 10. Sagebrush twigs have a complex branch structure and make good scale tree trunks. Without foliage they represent dead or dormant trees; just add Woodland Scenics netting material or lichen and they come alive.

PAINTING ROCKWORK AND PLASTER "SOIL"

Over the years I've tried many methods for coloring model railroad landscape. The best combination I've found so far, and the one I used on the J&S, is universal dyes and acrylic paints. I use the dyes to stain the rocks with basic coloring, then add a few brushloads of acrylic here and there on foreground rocks to give a little more vibrancy and richness to the color.

I first saw universal dyes used by Lonnie Shay and Paul Scoles on their narrow gauge

A. Carve trunk from ½"-square balsa

B. Rub on coarse sandpaper for bark effect

WHITE BURNT SIENNA

C. Stain with acrylic paints and lots of water

D. Poke holes with pin held in stick

E. Add caspia branches, using tweezers

FOAM

F. Spray branches with Pactra Earth. Let dry, then spray with Testor's Dullcote and sprinkle on ground-foam foliage

Fig. 11 BALSA/CASPIA PINE TREES

railroads. These dyes are used mainly to tint paints, so you'll find them at paint and hardware stores. Universals are easy to use, inexpensive, and they don't clog spray bottles. They're water-based but will mix with just about anything — that's why they're called universal, folks! They're quite forgiving, making mistakes nearly impossible.

As Paul and Lonnie told a crowded hobbyshop clinic audience one evening, "Even Olson can get usable results with universals." Kinda says it all.

When it came time to actually color the J&S, I used techniques taught me by Bob Jolley. Bob learned his trade in the Hollywood movie industry, painting and aging sets for movies ranging from *Cleopatra* to *The Great White Hope*.

I first met Bob in the mid-1970s. Since then we have worked together on building the two Big Thunder Mountain RR theme rides, one at Disneyland and the other at Walt Disney World. I supervised the construction and texturing of the rockwork, while Bob supervised painting and weathering the rocks and structures. The BTMRR's are really giant model railroads with mine trains carrying the guests over, under, and through Monument Valley-type scenery.

Let's get on with some Jolley-style rock coloring. Consult the lists of tools and materials.

Figure 2 shows our dyes ready to go. Mixing these colors reminds me of how we used to mix dyes to color Easter eggs when I was a kid. Put 10 ounces of water in each of the 10 tubs, add 15 to 20 drops of tint, and stir with a brush. My tints are Tints-All, available at Standard Brands paint stores and Ole's hardware stores. Equivalent products should be available in your area. The 1½ ounce tubes cost about $1 each, so $12 worth of tint will color several J&S-size layouts. Label each tub for the color it contains. Rinse the brush after each mixing.

Let's divide the work into foreground and background coloring.

FOREGROUND COLORING

Always paint your scenery under the type of lighting that will actually be used on the

layout. Colors can change amazingly with changes in lighting, particularly when going from incandescent to fluorescent lighting.

Figure 3 shows the steps in painting the foreground rocks. Use a 1" brush loaded with the desired color, and flood about 50 percent of the area you're working on in a random pattern. Remember, we're using the more vibrant colors — reds and browns in particular — in the foreground. Don't worry about slop; the color soaks in and will contribute to the overall effect. Be careful, however, to avoid distinct runs. You don't want sharp dividing lines between colors.

Next add the second color, overlapping the first and filling in more of the bare area remaining. I like to use three or four colors based on my real-world research, particularly my photographs. Always work toward your darker colors. You can't lighten your work without using white opaque acrylics.

◆ Fig 12. Effective tumbleweeds can be made from a synthetic horsehair scouring pad. First John sprays the green pad a rusty brown color; then he tears off small chunks. He rolls these between his fingers and teases up a few fibers.

Now we bring on the spray bottles, one filled with clear water, the other with a mix of raw umber (which is safest) or black. These colors *must* be very dilute so that you don't over darken the rock faces. Using the Jolley "twin six-shooters" method, blaze away with color from one hand, water from the other, alternating between the two and always keeping the dye in motion with the water wash.

Gravity works for you here. Most of the dark dye is washed away from the high areas, allowing the radiant first-color coats to show through where sunlight would normally strike. The dark wash accumulates in cracks, crevices, and lower areas, making them darker, pretty much as shadows would in the natural world. This wash process will also even out any excess blotchiness from the brushing operation.

Now use the acrylic tube colors — red oxide in this case — and carefully brush just a bit on the faces of the most prominent rock faces. Spray with water if you want a little blending. This step adds body to the paint job, going a little beyond the pastel look that dyes alone will yield. Acrylics are water-based, so you can do a lot with the spray bottle. Just don't go overboard and wash too much acrylic color down into the cracks and crevices. You could mask the dark shadows we added one step ago.

Now use just a bit of white acrylic and lightly dry-brush the highest relief and sky-facing edges of the rockwork. This will simulate the sunlit highlights that are usually missing in the much lower lighting levels of our train rooms. A little white goes a long way, so work with a very dry brush and back off 10 feet or so every now and then to check your progress.

The foreground rocks should now be rich in color with distinct variation in hues and values.

BACKGROUND COLORING

To simulate distance I colored the background scenery entirely with spray bottles, using only a few colors: yellow ochre followed with a random splash pattern of raw and burnt umber washes. The last was a dilute wash of pale blue to imply haze. Figure 4 shows the result. The rock on the left has a bit more color, as it's halfway between the foreground and background.

SOILS, GRAVEL, AND RUBBLE

My use of real earth and gravel dates back to my college days when my modeling budget was nonexistent. I took to gathering samples on my fishing trips to the High Sierra.

At first I was only filling empty beer cans, but then I got really hooked and moved up to 3-pound coffee cans. Once I began using the natural earths, I found they looked better than any synthetic material, were easy to apply, and automatically created alluvial fans and talus slopes. Ever since, I've used real materials extensively.

While gathering information and photos in Jerome, Ariz., I was also collecting dirt and weeds for the model railroad. Figure 5 shows me in action. In fig. 6 you can see my collection of dirt, gravel, as well as the strainers I use to sift these materials to four different scale grades: 1" particles and larger, 3/8" to 1" particles, sand to 3/8" particles, and fine sand.

A Styrofoam cup makes a perfectly serviceable dirt applicator. See fig. 7. I pour a

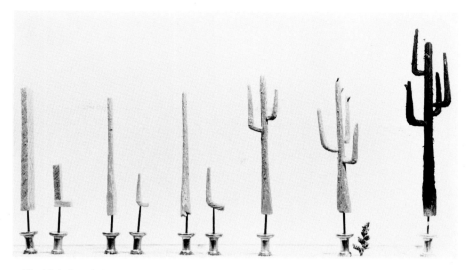

← Fig. 13. Left to right. Here's how to make those neat Saguaro cactuses that add so much personality to the J&S. Start with a 4"-long piece of 1/4"-square balsa for the main stem. From the same balsa make some L-shaped structures for arms. Carve these pieces to shape. John uses a no. 11 blade in an X-acto knife. Use 40 grit sandpaper, a razor saw blade, or a rough file to score in the characteristic deep vertical grooves. Glue the arms to the trunk. Clip a few caspia buds from a caspia branch and glue them on to represent blossoms. Paint the entire Saguaro Floquil Roof Brown and let it dry thoroughly. Dry-brush the corrugations with Depot Olive. Mix a little yellow with the green and dab it on here and there. Paint the blossoms yellow and add a bit of Caboose Red to snap-up the very tips.

thin coat of the desired color and grade of dirt onto the scenery, then brush it about to get the look I want, again using my research photos as a guide. You want some bare dirt areas, some graveled areas, boulder piles, and bare rock. Apply more and different grades of material until you get the results you want. Notice how the loose soil collects behind boulders and in depressions in natural repose.

Figure 7 also shows how I use a large, soft brush to maneuver the materials around and shape the soil. Note the narrow gauge

ties I have pressed into the loose soil. Most details such as barrels, tires, and junk should be pressed *into* the soil while it's workable instead of laid *on* a hard soil surface later.

I use a short, stiff-bristled brush to clear the flangeways of ballast and soil, being particularly careful around switch frogs, guardrails, and crossings.

MAKING IT STICK

Once I'm happy with the lay of the land, I wet it thoroughly, using a spray bottle

← Fig. 14. Pastel chalk powder between the rails represents oil and grease. To make powder John rubs the stick against coarse sandpaper. A light spray of Testors Dullcote will fix the chalk in place.

Fig. 15. Left. John didn't like his original canyon so he raised the floor with foam slabs, marking the wagon road before rough-shaping the terrain with a kitchen knife. Right. He covered the foam with a 50-50 mix of plaster and sawdust. Note the gaping hole in Cleopatra Hill. John sawed out the hillside and mailed it to friend Malcolm Furlow who built the mine to fit it. The attractive result of that Tom Sawyer episode is shown below.

full of water to which I've added 4 to 6 drops of liquid detergent. The detergent acts as a wetting agent, helping the water flow into the soil instead of causing it to ball up.

Once the ground is soaked, I apply a generous amount of dilute white glue to all the loose earth and ballast areas. An eyedropper will work fine, but using a spray bottle speeds the work and permits me to get glue into hard-to-reach places. I prefer a 3:1 ratio of water to glue. Again, a drop or two of liquid detergent helps the solution flow and seep into the wetted soil.

Sometimes puddles form on the surface, and the area just won't absorb more water. I simply sprinkle on a bit more fine dirt or dust to absorb the excess water.

After I've finished spraying glue, I wash away any excess from painted rock surfaces with a few squirts of clear water.

For good measure I add extra glue (50 percent water, 50 percent glue) along the track center line, using a squeeze bottle. This step will prevent any loose particles from getting into locomotive or rolling stock running gear, but more important, the extra glue will securely bond the track to the roadbed. I also use the squeeze bottle to saturate details like junk piles so they'll remain firmly on the layout.

When the glue has dried, the dirt and gravel will appear dry and loose. Often I return to an area after the soil has dried and overspray everything with a dilute umber or sienna wash to help tie the rocks and soil together.

Later, when you're adding trees and deadwood, you'll be using these same techniques to add small piles of sand or earth and blend the trunks into the landscape. I also use soils and gravel to hide a multitude of sins, gaps in the roadbed for exam-

ple, and trestle piers that don't quite reach the ground.

VEGETATION AND GROUND COVER

People often think of the desert as being barren, except for a rare cactus or two. Such is rarely the case and, as fig. 8 shows, it wasn't the case at Jerome.

All manner of things seems to grow out there, so we'll use a large variety of materials to represent them. We'll use natural weeds and bushes, and we'll also use some of the fine products from the hobby shop — lichen and ground foam, for example.

One good place to look for suitable plants is the local dried-flower boutique. Then when the season is right you can venture outdoors and see what's in the fields and along the roads. Be a little creative and open-minded and you'll find a wealth of material all around you. Figure 9 shows just a few of my favorites.

Sagebrush, because of its complex and dense branch structure, makes excellent tree trunks, as shown in fig. 10. The roots from sagebrush are also useful: they make good deadwood snags to place in hillside rock formations.

A foam block makes a good holder for your natural tree trunks while you're

Furlow's Folly Mine no. 1 is a rickety affair shoehorned into the side of towering Cleopatra Hill.

The mighty Saguaro cactus in the foreground of this photo goes a long way to establish the locale of the Jerome & Southwestern, but the rich variety of vegetation found everywhere on the layout is what makes the scenery alive and believable.

painting and adding foliage to them. Ground foam is particularly useful for dressing up weeds found in nature. You can spray small clumps of lichen, synthetic foliage, or dried plants with an adhesive (Testors Dullcote works especially well); or you can sprinkle on ground foam of various colors and degrees of coarseness, changing the character of your plants completely. Flock and electrostatic grass, available at hobby shops, are also good for dressing up foliage.

Figure 11 shows how I made my big pine trees, following basic techniques introduced by Jack Work 20 years ago. Tom Daniel showed me how to make those scouring pad tumbleweeds shown in fig. 12.

One plant the J&S cannot do without is the mighty Saguaro cactus. Figure 13 shows how I made them. I spent about one hour making the ten or so Saguaros on the J&S, and they've proved extremely popular with visitors.

FINISHING TOUCHES

Scenery should be weathered and aged just as structures and rolling stock should. Figure 14 shows how I brushed black chalk dust along the track center line to simulate accumulated oil and grease fallen from locomotives and cars. I applied it more heavily at service and station areas where locomotives spend more time.

I wanted driftwood and other debris in my stream bed, so I cemented it in while the creek was still dry. Then I poured the water into the creek, using polyester laminating resin. This is a material used for casting paperweights and encapsulating everything from butterflies to pennies. You'll find it sold in most craft shops. I poured properly catalyzed batches ¼" deep at a time, let each pour cure 24 hours, then repeated until I had the depth I wanted.

There's no law saying you can't change scenery after you finish it. As fig. 15 shows, I didn't care for the canyon as first built, so I changed it.

That wraps up our stint on scenery. J&S country is now so alive and inviting that we can expect an influx of people wanting to live and work there. Next we'll set about providing some homes and businesses for them.

Structures
for the Jerome & Southwestern

Painting and weathering techniques for buildings with personality

The 4 x 8-foot HO Jerome & Southwestern appears enormous when we look across it with the Back Alley & Wharf addition as a background. (Building the BA&W is described in Chapter 9.) Author Olson built most of his structures from plastic kits.

THE Jerome & Southwestern now looks like a finished model railroad, and that's good because we've come to that part of layout building that goes slowly. There's no way you can rush your structures and be happy with the results. They simply take a lot of time.

On the other hand structures are tremendously satisfying projects. You can be extremely creative in approaching them. You can scratchbuild any kind of structure you want, but you also have a tremendous selection of kits from which to choose. A good hobby shop will have ready-built plastic buildings costing only a few dollars on one shelf, while right next to them on another shelf will be craftsman kits of museum quality costing many tens of dollars and requiring weeks of hobby time to build.

You can build any of these kits exactly as the directions say, or you can modify them so they fit your situation and ideas more closely. No one has ever been strung up for departing from the directions, only for ignoring them altogether. Also, you can combine two or more kits or parts of kits to create unique structures of your own design, a process usually called kitbashing.

Figure 1 lists the kits I used on the Jerome & Southwestern. Chances are good you'll want to use many of these same kits, but I hope you'll also try some different structures and ideas of your own. Capturing the spirit is far more important than duplicating the list. Besides, I think some of the kits I used have been out of production for quite a while. You see, I'm a hoarder. When I see kits I like I buy them; sometimes I don't get around to using them for years.

By the way, bridges are structures too, and you'll notice I kitbashed most of mine from a variety of inexpensive kits. Figure 2 shows the long bridge that crosses above Clarkdale. I built it as one unit that can easily be removed, a handy feature both for maintenance and photographic reasons.

Assembling kits is simple, but making truly beautiful and realistic structures is a matter of mastering effective painting and weathering techniques. In this installment of the J&S story I want to take you through the construction and painting of a typical, inexpensive plastic kit, sharing with you the techniques I use. To illustrate the project, I suggest that we use the Atlas signal tower, kit no. 704.

WHY THIS PARTICULAR KIT?

I'm glad you asked. This is a great old kit with a wealth of cast-on detail. It's a kit typical of those generally used by beginners

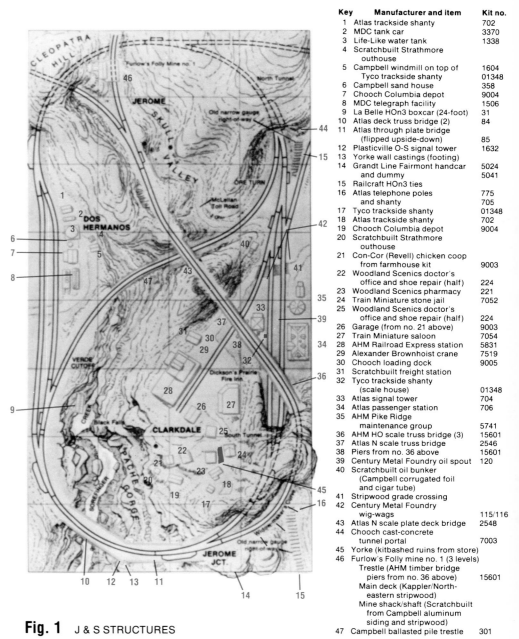

Fig. 1 J & S STRUCTURES

Key	Manufacturer and item	Kit no.
1	Atlas trackside shanty	702
2	MDC tank car	3370
3	Life-Like water tank	1338
4	Scratchbuilt Strathmore outhouse	
5	Campbell windmill on top of	1604
	Tyco trackside shanty	01348
6	Campbell sand house	358
7	Chooch Columbia depot	9004
8	MDC telegraph facility	1506
9	La Belle HOn3 boxcar (24-foot)	31
10	Atlas deck truss bridge (2)	84
11	Atlas through plate bridge (flipped upside-down)	85
12	Plasticville O-S signal tower	1632
13	Yorke wall castings (footing)	
14	Grandt Line Fairmont handcar	5024
	and dummy	5041
15	Railcraft HOn3 ties	
16	Atlas telephone poles	775
	and shanty	705
17	Tyco trackside shanty	01348
18	Atlas trackside shanty	702
19	Chooch Columbia depot	9004
20	Scratchbuilt Strathmore outhouse	
21	Con-Cor (Revell) chicken coop from farmhouse kit	9003
22	Woodland Scenics doctor's office and shoe repair (half)	224
23	Woodland Scenics pharmacy	221
24	Train Miniature stone jail	7052
25	Woodland Scenics doctor's office and shoe repair (half)	224
26	Garage (from no. 21 above)	9003
27	Train Miniature saloon	7054
28	AHM Railroad Express station	5831
29	Alexander Brownhoist crane	7519
30	Chooch loading dock	9005
31	Scratchbuilt freight station	
32	Tyco trackside shanty (scale house)	01348
33	Atlas signal tower	704
34	Atlas passenger station	706
35	AHM Pike Ridge maintenance group	5741
36	AHM HO scale truss bridge (3)	15601
37	Atlas N scale truss bridge	2546
38	Piers from no. 36 above	15601
39	Century Metal Foundry oil spout	120
40	Scratchbuilt oil bunker (Campbell corrugated foil and cigar tube)	
41	Stripwood grade crossing	
42	Century Metal Foundry wig-wags	115/116
43	Atlas N scale plate deck bridge	2548
44	Chooch cast-concrete tunnel portal	7003
45	Yorke (kitbashed ruins from store)	
46	Furlow's Folly mine no. 1 (3 levels) Trestle (AHM timber bridge piers from no. 36 above)	15601
	Main deck (Kappler/Northeastern stripwood)	
	Mine shack/shaft (Scratchbuilt from Campbell aluminum siding and stripwood)	
47	Campbell ballasted pile trestle	301

Fig. 2. John built the big bridge over Clarkdale by combining pieces from inexpensive plastic kits.

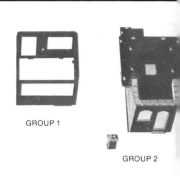

GROUP 1

GROUP 2

Fig. 4. After familiarizing himself with the tower's parts, John laid them out in five groups for initial painting with an airbrush.

◆ Fig. 3. In this installment John demonstrates his painting and weathering techniques while building this Atlas signal tower. It's a great learner's kit.

and intermediate modelers, but some veterans think of kits like this as being too toylike. That's one reason I chose it for our demonstrator. With a little creative painting and the addition of just a few details, we can have a model that will look right at home on the veteran scratchbuilder's pike.

Another thing — you can gain a variety of experience with this one kit because it includes four different simulated construction materials: brick, wood, metal, and tile. I'll show you how to finish each of these so it looks like the real thing.

Oh, one last thing — if your initial efforts are disappointing, you aren't out much, only a few bucks and a few hours. Just wait until no one is looking, chuck your building in the scrap box (pieces of it may come in handy later), and go out and buy another kit. Try, try again.

FIRST STEPS

Figure 3 shows my completed signal tower. Eventually I placed it under the bridge at Clarkdale. If you were to build the tower without painting it, you'd have it together in less than an hour. My painted and weathered version took about five times that long.

I studied the directions and used them as a guide, but I didn't follow them to the letter. For example, I left off the base because it simulates soil, an item better represented by real soil, as described in our last installment. Once I had familiarized myself with the parts, I sorted them into five

groups to simplify the painting. See fig. 4. Painting as you go, rather than trying to paint the finished model, is the key to good results.

Notice that I assembled the brick and wood walls into their respective boxes before painting them. Here are some assembly tips — these may be old hat, but they're still mighty important.

● Carefully trim the parts from the casting sprues with a sharp hobby knife, as shown in fig. 5. Never twist or break the parts from their sprues.

● Use a liquid solvent type of cement, as shown in fig. 6. The liquid is much easier to control and much less messy than the tube type. Dip a no. 1 sable brush into the solvent; then touch it to the pieces you

◀ Fig. 5. John uses a knife to cut parts from sprues.

◀ Fig. 6. Liquid cement is neater than the tube-type.

◀ Fig. 7. Real brick is seldom uniformly colored, so John mixes up batches of lighter and darker reds and brushes them randomly on the walls to create a fairly subtle range of hues.

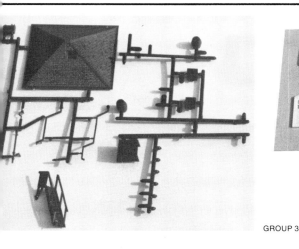

GROUP 4

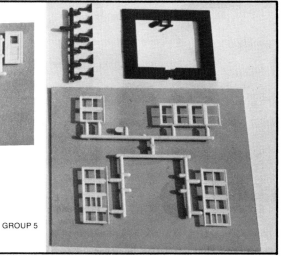

GROUP 3   GROUP 5

wish to join. Capillary action will pull the solvent into the joint automatically.

• Use the solvent only in a well-ventilated area — the fumes are toxic. Once you master liquid cement, you will never return to the tube type!

I airbrushed the five groups with Floquil paints. To the roof and other details in Group 1 I applied a coat of gray primer to serve as a base for brush detailing later. I gave the wooden walls in Group 2 a light base coat of Roof Brown, then after 30 minutes' drying time, a top coat of Reefer Yellow. I applied a base coat of Caboose Red to the brick walls and chimney in Group 3. For the lower-level windows and doors in Group 4 I used Reefer White. The upper-level floor, roof braces, window frames, and door in Group 5 got a shot of Boxcar Red. I let all these painted pieces cure for one day.

FINISHING BRICK

Now we go to work on our brick walls. Real bricks are seldom uniformly colored,

← Fig. 8. Spackling compound is great mortar.

← Fig. 9. John brushes the yellow walls with solvent until the brown base coat shows through.

so our first step is to introduce some color variation, thus adding character and avoiding a too-clean, toylike finish.

Mix a small batch of lighter red by adding Reefer White to Caboose Red; also mix a batch of darker red by adding a little Grimy Black to Caboose Red. For a dirty red, whip up yet another batch using more Grimy Black.

Using a brush, apply these colors randomly to achieve a mottled look, as shown in fig. 7. The brushed-on colors can even overlap each other from time to time. Random variation is the key in this process.

Once the paint dries (several days), I like to bring out the mortar lines. As fig. 8 shows, I use a water-dampened rag to rub DAP brand spackling compound into the brick joints. I try to keep most of the DAP in the joints, with only a little getting over onto the brick faces.

I used the pure white here, but you can tint the DAP to a gray or concrete color by adding a little black poster or water paint. Spackling compound is easy to control, much easier than the white paint that is often used, and you can wash it off entirely with water and an old toothbrush if you decide to start over.

Once the DAP is dry I wipe off any excess that has gotten into areas where it doesn't belong. Don't worry if the DAP's appearance is too stark to suit you. You can mute it easily with a thin wash of paint.

AGED AND PEELING WOOD

The first step in aging our wood clapboard is to brush lightly along the boards with a thinner-laden brush, as shown in fig. 9. Do this randomly, backing off as soon as the yellow top coat softens and the brown base coat begins to show through in a few areas. This simulates the wood itself showing through worn paint.

Subtle variations in color and aging are easy to achieve if you work slowly. Keep in mind that rain, dirt, and sunlight combine to vary the shades of color. Wall areas less exposed to the elements, like those under the eaves, will show less aging. Those more exposed will be bleached and highlighted by the sun and the elements.

Let the paint harden for several days before proceeding to the next step. Again working parallel with the boards, scrape here and there with a sharp X-acto knife

until the top coat of paint begins to chip and peel away. See fig. 10. Try for varying degrees of chip and peel, with the most damage occuring in exposed areas away from the protection of eaves and gables. Look at real buildings around your town for references.

HIGHLIGHTING SHINGLES

Effectively painted roofs are extremely important because on most layouts we're looking down on the buildings. Here I'll describe painting techniques to simulate two important effects: strong sunlight and aging.

Most rooms where model railroads are built have lighting levels far lower than those found out-of-doors. The eye strain would be terrific if we lighted our miniature worlds as intensely as the sun lights the real one.

Frequently we use flourescent lamps because of their even lighting characteristics.

← Fig. 10. Some scraping with an X-acto knife creates the look of chipping and peeling paint.

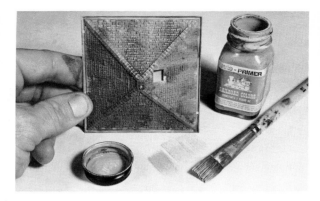

◆ Fig. 11. Left to right. Step one in finishing the roof is painting it with a brush dipped in Roof Brown and thinner. Next John brushes on a thin tan, evening out the mottled look a bit in the process. He finishes by dry-brushing with gray primer. In effect he's painted in the highlights and shadows that would be created by sunlight.

These same characteristics, however, cause a lack of shadows, hence a lack of definition, on model surfaces, most notably roofs. Using an occasional spotlight in the room lighting system will help to some degree, but the most effective way to attain the look of sunlight striking our models is with subtly painted highlights.

Just as the landscape artist can add lighting to his painting, we can add lighting to our models, and quite easily too, as we are usually working on three dimensional surfaces. Take your Atlas roof outdoors in strong sunlight and you can really appreciate the excellent job they've done with the mold work to make a realistic shingled roof.

Figure 11 shows how to highlight all that beautiful detail with paint. First arm yourself with a bottle of Floquil Roof Brown, some Floquil Dio-Sol thinner, and a ½"-wide flat brush. Load the brush with thinner; then just touch it to the inside of the paint jar cap to put some full-strength paint on the tips of the bristles. Now quickly touch the brush to the roof and streak downward to the rain gutter. Go back to the thinner with the brush, then touch to the roof. This second application will be a bit lighter than the first, producing some variation. Work around the roof one panel at a time. This procedure simulates shadows under and alongside the shingles. The blotchy look is just what you want. Let the roof dry for a day or so.

Our next step is adding an aged wood color to the roof. Use the same brush and some Depot Buff or Earth diluted heavily with thinner. As you apply it, strive for a somewhat patchy appearance. This step will moderate the bold patchiness of the previous step, yet not even it out as a spray coat would. Refer again to fig. 11. The original light-gray base coat will still show through enough to keep the roof from being too dark.

The last step adds sunlight and dimension to the shingles. For this we will use the dry-brush technique. Dip the brush into the primer color, then wipe the bristles against the top inside of the jar to remove as much paint as possible. Stroke the brush back and forth on a piece of paper until very little paint is being transferred to the paper.

Now stroke the roof lightly, working from the rain gutter up towards the peak, using short, rapid strokes. Notice how only the raised lower edges of the shingles pick up paint. The highlights really show up well against the Roof Brown that has collected in the crevices and cracks.

Complete the roof by painting the gutters silver and dappling on a bit of rust. Glue in the chimney and streak just a hint of Boxcar Red paint or Sienna pastel chalk down the roof from the chimney toward the gutter, simulating streaks from rain and age.

PAINTING DETAILS

For easy handling I paint the small detail parts on their sprues. Remember, we've already primed these parts. I apply the color coat using either wash or dry-brush techniques, depending on the situation. Here's a good rule of thumb: If the color coat is darker than the primer coat, flow on a dilute wash so it will run into the cracks and crevices, thus emphasizing the detail. If, on the other hand, the color coat is lighter than the primer, use the dry-brush method to highlight the raised detail areas.

ASSEMBLY TECHNIQUES

I like to build my structures in subassemblies, completing the detail on each before combining them to make the finished structure. Subassemblies are easier to handle than the entire building when it comes to detailing and painting. Also, the less I handle the whole building, the less likely I am to drop it or damage it in some other way. Figure 12 shows the two major subassemblies for this tower kit.

Windows are the building's eyes, you might say. How you treat them goes a long way towards establishing the building's personality. The window shades for our signal tower are printed on the acetate, but if they weren't, we'd certainly want to add them. As fig. 13 shows, I added break lines to one of my windows by scratching the break pattern onto the proper area of the acetate window material.

I trimmed my window material to size and glued it to the window frames before

Fig. 15. To add vines, John applies white glue, then sprinkles on ground foam and pats it in.

◆ Fig. 13. To impart personality to his tower, John carved break lines into one window pane.

◆ Fig. 14. John uses a cyanoacrylate cement, Hot Stuff in this instance, to attach acetate windows.

Fig. 12. John approached the structure as two main subassemblies. It's easier to detail and weather smaller units and less damage will occur if a unit is dropped.

installing it in the wall. As shown in fig. 14, I used Hot Stuff for this step and prepared all the windows at one time, making for a clean and speedy installation.

ADDING VINES AND WEEDS

Vines will give any building that lived-in look, and they take only a few minutes to add.

First draw on the vine pattern with white glue. As fig. 15 shows, I use a needle-type probe, working fast so the glue won't have time to skin over.

Sprinkle ground foam, like that offered by Woodland Scenics, over the glue pattern and pat it down gently with your fingers. Variety in colors and textures is important — I used two different shades of green in three sizes to make the vine on the signal tower. Your vines will look artificial if they are too uniform. You might want to try using a fine grade of dark foam for a first coat, then coming back over it with the brighter, coarser foam to represent new

growth. Experiment with different sequences to find combinations you like. After an hour or so brush off the loose foam and save it to use again.

We often see weeds and tall grass growing right next to the foundation of a building. A good source for these plants is moss or ferns bought at a dried-flower or craft shop. Glue these bits of moss directly against the side of the building, using white glue and tweezers, as shown in fig. 16. It's easier to add these at the workbench, so don't wait until your model has been placed permanently on the layout.

At last it's time to plant our structure, using real soil and the techniques explained in the last installment. We don't want any gaps between the foundation and the soil, and we want our building to look as if it's been there awhile. Here are some tricks that help: add a few trees and shrubs along the sides, place details like ladders and boards leaning against the walls, connect a fence to the building.

TAKE YOUR TIME

Practice, practice, practice. You'll find that the painting and finishing techniques you've developed while building some of the simpler plastic buildings will serve you well on those kitbashing, craftsman kit, or scratchbuilding projects in which you've invested many more hours.

Take your time and enjoy structure building. After all, because you've covered the ground with basic scenery materials the layout looks complete. Each new structure will make everything else look a little different, introducing a refreshing change for you and your friends.

By now you've undoubtedly been running some trains on your version of the Jerome & Southwestern, and you've been having fun doing it. In the next chapter we'll look at ways to add personality to ready-made rolling stock, and then we'll make those plastic engines and cars really come alive!

Fig. 16. It's easiest to add weeds before permanently installing the structure on the layout.

A few weatherbeaten structures are all it takes to establish a tank town like Dos Hermanos as an important stop on the J&S. Human figures are an often overlooked detail that adds life to any layout.

Locomotives and cars for the Jerome & Southwestern

Techniques for detailing and weathering rolling stock with personality

TRAINS MOVE; that's why they contribute so much to the magic of our model railroads. In fact, motion has a lot to do with the built-in realism of model railroad equipment. It's not hard to imagine that the train is the real thing when we can watch intently as one by one each car is tugged into motion and our train pulls slowly away from the station. Our eyes follow as the train swings bravely across a high, frail bridge. Somewhere along the line we lose our sense of the train's actual size. The moving train draws us into the scene and imparts life to our miniature world; without its motion we'd be left with a static diorama. Because the trains themselves contribute so much to the railroad's personality, we want them to run extremely well and we want them to look good while doing it. Looking good and running good — those are our subjects in this chapter.

SCALE APPEARANCE

Scale appearance is often thought of as properly sized wheel flanges, grab irons, and such, but here I'm thinking more of how natural and at home locomotives and cars look

Imagine how out-of-the-box, shiny ore cars would spoil this scene. Scale appearance is a matter of everything looking as if it belongs. Besides, it's lots of fun to beat up and weather model railroad equipment.

in a layout scene. Nothing spoils the illusion more quickly than shiny, unweathered locomotives and cars in the middle of a nicely detailed and realistic-looking layout. Here are three rules of thumb I think will help us avoid creating toylike models.

• Never use straight black on a car or locomotive; mix it down with 5 to 10 percent white. In the low light levels of our layout rooms, details just don't show on truly black models; they become black holes in our miniature landscapes. Look at black diesels in service or color photos of steamers and notice how gray they usually appear. Save true black for representing oil spills.

• Tone down brightly colored car kits with an *ultra* thin overspray of gray primer, followed by Floquil Dust. Also lightly spray the trucks and undercarriage with Grimy Black. This will kill the shine, show off the details, and amounts to scaling the paint job by putting the range of colors and finishes into the range found in nature.

• Aging and weathering your equipment is the most important step of all. I figure the equipment on a bite-and-kick outfit like the J&S takes a real beating, so I give it the works. After all, in the desert it can be 120 in the day and 10 below at night. Sandstorms, rain, snow, and anything else Ma Nature cares to toss at rail equipment takes its toll. Metal rusts, paint fades and peels, soot and grime accumulate. Man gets in his licks with spilled lubricants, spot painting, and restenciling. All these effects can be simulated with the two basic methods I'll describe next. Most of the time I use both.

AGING WITH WASHES

I like to age models by flowing on thin washes of paint and lacquer thinner. Figure 1 shows typical results. Floquil is the paint brand I almost always use. There's only one problem with this method, but it's a big one: If you make a mistake it's Boot Hill for the car! Lacquer thinner can dissolve the decals, paint, and even the plastic car itself! The secret is working only a short time on any one particular part of the car, so you don't break through the paint coat that protects the plastic.

The basic technique is to flood a wash of very thin paint onto the car, then let it run down. I use a ¼"-wide (or wider) flat brush to avoid a striped look. To get only a little color on the brush, I touch it against the inside of the cap, rather than dipping into

Fig. 1. John uses washes of paint and lacquer thinner to achieve weathering effects like the stains and streaks on the side of this reefer. Some pastel chalk work is also apparent on the truck and end.

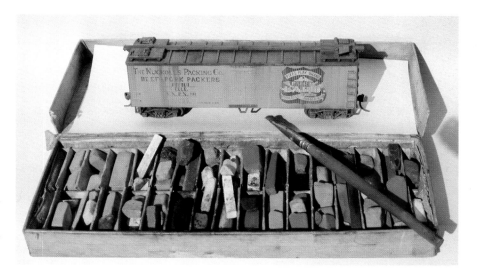

Fig. 2. Pastel chalks come in dozens of colors. John scrubs them on with stiff brushes. They can be washed off if he doesn't like the effect. Once satisfied he fixes them with clear, flat spray finishes.

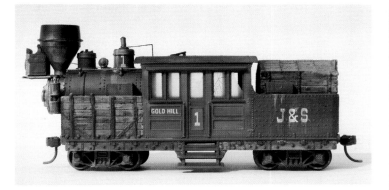

Fig. 3. The Jerome & Southwestern certainly has a varied motive power roster! Here we see the two extremes. John pulled out all the stops in aging no. 1, a Roundhouse Climax, shown above. The Athearn SW1500, right, is the J&S's most modern engine. John weathered it to look hard-working but well-maintained.

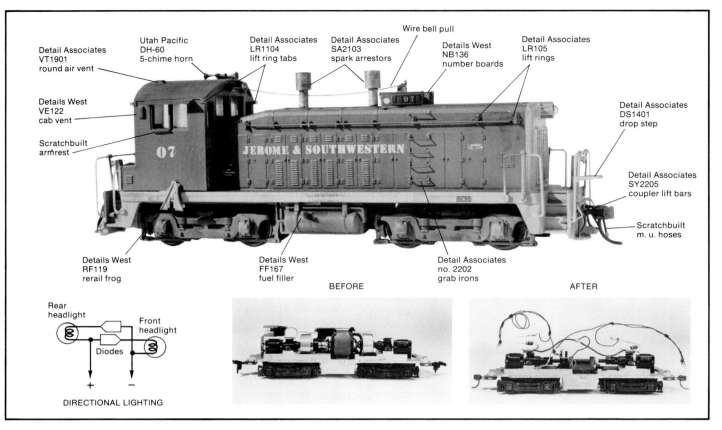

Detail Associates
VT1901
round air vent

Utah Pacific
DH-60
5-chime horn

Detail Associates
LR1104
lift ring tabs

Detail Associates
SA2103
spark arrestors

Wire bell pull

Details West
NB136
number boards

Detail Associates
LR105
lift rings

Details West
VE122
cab vent

Detail Associates
DS1401
drop step

Scratchbuilt
armrest

Detail Associates
SY2205
coupler lift bars

Details West
RF119
rerail frog

Details West
FF167
fuel filler

Detail Associates
no. 2202
grab irons

Scratchbuilt
m. u. hoses

BEFORE

AFTER

Rear
headlight

Front
headlight

Diodes

+   −

DIRECTIONAL LIGHTING

Fig. 4. John gave his SW1500 a personality all its own by adding lots of detail parts. As the before and after shots of the chassis show, he also added a Proto Power West drive and a bidirectional lighting system.

the bottle itself. I alternately touch the brush to the color and dip it into the thinner as I work. Since we are using a lot of solvent in this process, work in a well-ventilated area only.

On most cars I begin by washing a black or gray thinner solution from the roof's center line to the eave. Then I work from the eave to the bottom of the side.

Next I add complementary color washes. If, for example, I am working on an orange refrigerator car, I will now come back with a little orange, then yellow, to add variation to the base color. Since you're simulating the action of rain as it washes away dead paint, stains the surface, and deposits grit, it's important to work perfectly vertical from top to bottom. Use only one stroke to complete the distance. If the paint becomes too striped or garish, you can flow a brushload of solvent over the area and blow it dry.

For the sake of variety, you can also use watercolor washes on your equipment. They give nice results, drying to a chalky appearance, and if you don't like the results you can just wash them off with no harm done.

PASTEL CHALKS

Figure 2 shows one of my favorite weathering media, chalks. You're gonna love these! They go on quick and easy and the effects are easy to control. Any artist supply store carries inexpensive sets with basic earth tones and a few colors, but I prefer to spend a few bucks more and get all the greens, yellows, blues, oranges, and reds as well.

The earth tones are great for simulating grime and dirt as it builds up on a car, but the different shades of primary color are

useful for representing variations in the color coat itself. On a green car, for example, I might represent faded paint by scrubbing in lighter greens and yellows. I might use darker greens and blues under the eaves, with paler tones on the more exposed surfaces. These variations should be kept subtle, but wow! do they ever lend to the believability of a model.

Here's how to use chalks. Take a ¼"-wide flat brush with its bristles trimmed ⅛" long. Scrub the brush on the chalk stick, then scrub an area on the model. Notice how the rivets and other details suddenly stand out. Use the grime and dirt and soot colors first. Then go back and vary the car color itself a bit. You'll have to practice to get the results you want, but anytime you're not satisfied you can wash the chalk right off and start over.

Once you're satisfied, seal the car with Testor's Dullcote, Micro Scale's Microcoat Flat, or some other flat lacquer. If too much chalk disappears during the sealing process, just add more chalk and seal the surface again.

One trick I like is to use Micro Flat as the sealer. It stays tacky for an hour or so and I scrub chalks right into the tacky surface. The chalk won't rub off, yet retains its dry, flaky, oxidized look.

PAINTING THE J&S LOCOMOTIVES

I wanted to have some fun with the J&S motive power roster, and there's probably never been a more varied accumulation of engines run on any railroad anywhere. I figure the J&S bought their engines used from anyone desperate enough to accept a typical J&S offer. After all, this outfit would have rustled their motive power if

they'd thought they could get away with it!

I wanted my engines to show off a full range of aging effects. Figure 3 shows engines at each end of the spectrum. The Climax is in sorry shape; the diesel, by J&S standards, looks terrific.

I made few physical modifications to these locomotives, giving them their personalities almost entirely through the application of paints. It's the variety of colors and aging effects that separate them from their fresh-off-the-shelf brethren. The painting and weathering techniques I used on the Roundhouse Climax are essentially the same as those I used on the other steamers, differing only in degree, so let me take you through it.

GOOD OLD NO. 1

Old no. 1, shown in fig. 3, is a Roundhouse Climax. Her name's *Gold Hill*, but you never hear her called that around the J&S. Everybody looks out for old no. 1, so I wanted it to be a dandy, a derelict that looked ready for, if not already on, the rip track. I had only a few bucks invested in this unpowered engine, so I decided to empty out the whole bag of tricks, from broken glass to rust holes.

The kit comes with lots of optional parts, so by choosing different types of stacks and such, you can alter the engine's looks a good deal. Once all the valves, pumps, and other important-looking details have been added, the little teapot is ready for painting.

I airbrushed the body shell with a 10:1 Floquil Grimy Black and Reefer White mixture and let it dry several days. Then I dabbed Zinc Chromate Primer on the cab roof until most of the surface was covered in a mottled pattern representing peeling and flaking paint. After this paint had dried a few minutes, I dry-brushed random patches of Roof Brown and Rust on the roof to simulate both old and freshly rusted areas.

Next, using Flo-Stain Driftwood, I brush-painted the wooden fuel box and the wood within it. After it had dried, I dry-brushed the box itself with oak stain, giving it an aged look. For contrast I dry-brushed the logs in the box with Earth, making them look fresh-cut. These warm tones also helped separate the organic wooden parts from the cooler metallic parts.

I stained the cab sides and front with a very dilute wash of Depot Green. Later these sides were dusted with green pastel chalks to achieve a dry look.

With a small brush I carefully painted the window and door frames Tuscan Red. Small touches like this imply a happier past when the locomotive was better cared for.

For window glass I used .020″-thick clear acetate. The broken windowpane was accomplished by deft use of an X-acto knife with a no. 11 blade. The dirty or frosty look of the windows came from a light misting, using Micro Flat in an airbrush. This light misting also protects the pastel chalks during handling.

Speaking of chalks, be careful when you're using them heavily, as in a case like this, that you don't use too many colors. You don't want a strident, painted-lady look. You can blend the colors subtly by using a large brush in a light scrubbing motion.

I airbrushed a little Engine Black along the top of the locomotive from the stack rearward. This represents the soot that falls out of the smoke and is an important touch on all the J&S steam engines.

Once I'd installed Kadee couplers I was able to couple this dummy into any train and let it work as a helper engine. If I should want to power the Climax, all I have to do is snap it over Model Die Casting's boxcab diesel chassis.

DETAILING THE ATHEARN SW1500

I'd never done much with diesels, but once I got started I found they had just as much character as the steamers I was used to — I'd just never known how to recognize it. Two sources set me straight real fast on these newfangled growlers that had always looked so simple to an old teapot modeler like me.

First I stopped in at a hobby shop, the Little Depot in Anaheim, Calif. Friend, clerk, and fellow modeler, Craig Walker, provided color rail postcards from Vanishing Vistas and Rail Card, the current issue of TRAINS Magazine, and an hour's worth of advice on what makes a diesel tick. As far as I'm concerned this is what a good hobby shop is all about — reliable information coupled with the latest products and techniques for using them.

My second research source was a quick trip to the nearest grade crossing to watch a few diesels rumble and growl past. My appetite now properly whetted, I made a shopping list of detail parts, formulated a plan of attack, and modified the common Athearn SW1500 into J&S no. 07.

The most significant modification came with cutting the stock smokestacks off and adding the Detail Associates stacks with spark arrestors. All the other details were simply glued on. Figure 4 shows the details I added. The packages that detail parts come in usually have information on where and how to attach them.

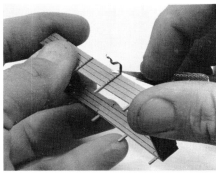

◄ Fig. 5. Top to bottom. John wanted his Roundhouse ore cars to look like battle-scarred but victorious veterans. Tapping on the steel sides with a soldering iron created the look of metal that has been pounded back into shape with a sledgehammer. The Floquil paint John used to retouch the sides attacked and crazed the raw plastic a bit, making the car look even better! John scraped the top extension boards with a razor saw to represent the pronounced wood grain caused by natural sand blasting to which J&S equipment is often subjected. He distressed the wood further with an X-acto knife. The finished car looks well used, but far from used up.

I scratchbuilt the window shades and armrests from bits of .010″-thick styrene. My m.u. hoses are small-diameter motor hookup wire inserted into holes drilled in the end beams. These details add a lot and cost only a penny or two.

After all the glued-on details had cured for a day, I airbrushed the locomotive body Grimy Black. I let the Grimy Black cure for a day, then masked the body with Scotch Tape and airbrushed the end platforms, radiator housing, and chassis frame D&RGW yellow.

As I'd done with all the steamers, I dab-painted the cab roof with zinc chromate primer. This touch lends a family look to the stable.

I kept the aging moderate to indicate hard service with regular maintenance. The J&S runs hard, but keeps on running!

ORE CARS THAT HAVE BEEN AROUND

The Jerome & Southwestern ore trains are a regular museum of older and second-hand equipment. The wooden boards are often split, broken, or just plain missing, while the metal parts are usually bent, dinged up, and corroded. These effects are easy to create in plastic models. Let's use the Roundhouse 3-in-1 Wood Chip car kit no. 1501 for our demonstration. See fig. 5.

To give the steel car sides that well-used look, first heat the walls by holding a 40-watt, large-tip soldering iron inside the car. Then press a screwdriver or other tool against the softened wall to make dents and creases, both inside and out. When you try it, watch that the side ribs don't bend too much during heating. You want a car that looks banged up, not melted! Work in a well-ventilated area — the smoke produced can't be good for you.

Next I take a small, pencil-tipped soldering iron and pat rapidly on the outside of the car to represent steel that has been pounded back into shape by the shop crews. Finally, I use a knife and small file to scrape and dress up any melted-looking areas.

Since I prefer to glue the body and frame together, I file the snap tabs off the frame. I finish assembling the basic car, then paint it Boxcar Red. After several days' drying time I wash on a few variations of dilute Boxcar Red mixed with Grimy Black.

So much for representing banged-up steel. Now to make plastic look like wood. I assemble the side boards as per the kit instructions and let them dry overnight.

Wanting my boards to look thoroughly battered and ready for replacement, I really give them the treatment. First I use a razor saw and scrape along the length of the boards to simulate exposed wood grain. I also do this to the inside surfaces if I'm not planning to add a load. The tip of the saw is good for touching up a few boards individually so the grain on all four boards won't be perfectly parallel.

Next I use an X-acto knife with a sharp no. 11 blade to trim the edges between some boards and carve in some splits and knotholes. I make sure to eliminate the straight line along the tops of the sides, since that's where the most damage occurs — some of the rocks being loaded don't quite hit the mark.

I paint the side boards with Gray primer, then add a dilute wash of Oak. It's important to the car's character that the wood parts be clearly distinquishable from the steel.

● Fig. 6. Left to right. John had his private roadname decals custom-made. After soaking them off the backing paper he applied them carefully to the moistened car side, using tweezers. Next he snugged them into position using a setting solution. After the protective flat finish coat had been sprayed

● Fig. 7. Clockwise. Adding coal loads was easy as one, two, three. First John cut and fit a false floor made from illustration board. After white-gluing it in place, he added the coal, mounding it in two to four piles to appear as if it had been loaded from multiple chutes. Next he wet the coal with detergent-laced water from a spray bottle, then fixed it in position with a 1:1 solution of water and white glue, applied with a squeeze bottle.

DECALS WITH PERSONALITY

Among the things that contribute most to a railroad's personality are its name and its herald. Inventing names and designing heralds is fun, but obviously you can't go down to your local hobby shop and buy decals for a railroad that exists only in your imagination. I solved this problem by having a custom decal maker, Custom Screen & Decal Co., make my decals for me. Several companies offer this service and advertise in MODEL RAILROADER.

Figure 6 shows the steps in applying decals, as well as measures I sometimes take to weather and distress the lettering so it matches the rest of the car. Usually I don't go as far as I did here, but often I do spend a little time brushing thinner over the decals, causing the ink to begin to dissolve and streak downward. You can get great effects this way, but go slowly and carefully. Sometimes these things work, and sometimes they don't. Experiment. If you see signs of trouble, stop immediately and let the car dry for a day. Usually the damage, if any, isn't nearly as bad as you thought it'd be. In fact, it usually looks good!

You don't have to start with an unpainted car every time you want to letter one for your own railroad. Often you can rub away the prepainted herald and road name with a Q-tip and decal-setting solution, then add your own markings. I've also been able to carefully scratch old markings away with an X-acto knife.

Sometimes prototype railroads replace worn lettering by first spot-painting the area where the lettering goes and then stenciling on new letters. You can simulate this process easily by masking a lettered area with tape, then weathering the car as we've done earlier. When you pull away the tape, the clean area will look newly painted.

CAR LOADS

Adding loads to your hoppers and gondolas gives them purpose. Each type of load — coal, ballast, ore, whatever — tells a different story about where the car came from or might be going.

I make a false floor for these open cars so I don't use up all my coal on one load or make the car too heavy. Foam blocks and cardboard floors are easy to use and cost next to nothing. Figure 7 shows the steps

● Fig. 8. John represents oil spills with black paint straight from the bottle. Clear gloss on parts of some spills gives them a fresh look. Other spill areas may be dull and have collected dirt and dust.

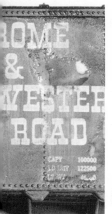

n and was dry, John brushed on a wash of gray primer and thinner, carrying right down over the decal. Next he got adventurous and allowed a pool of thinner to lay over the lettering and evaporate. Once dry the effect was striking and rather similar to nature's artistic efforts on this prototype Frisco car.

in adding a coal load, but you don't have to make your own. Roller Bearing, McLeod, and Model Dynamics all make loads for hoppers and gondolas that look good and snap right in. Soda straws are great for pipe loads and tinfoil scraps work well in a scrap iron gondola. Stakes, coils of rope, chains, and chock blocks on flatcars — all these indicate recent use. Trucks, farm vehicles, or even out-of-service railroad cars also make interesting loads.

There are other neat ways to show your cars are actually being used. Add graffiti on the car sides with a white pencil or fine brush and white paint. Cut small pieces of paper and cement them to the doors or tackboards to indicate car orders, repair orders, or lading restrictions.

As fig. 8 shows, you can add oil spills to tank cars, making them look fresh or old as the spirit moves you. Scratches on boxcar sides, like those shown in fig. 9, suggest that HO people have been opening and closing the door. And speaking of people, they're the most important details of all when it comes to adding life to your equipment.

I put crews in all my locomotives, and I also like to add brakemen riding the footboards, crewmen lounging on caboose platforms, and some folks just hitching rides on flatcars or in open boxes. You don't need enough people to fill a football stadium, but at the same time it's hard to have too many.

GOOD OPERATION

At the beginning I said we'd also talk a bit about performance. Good running starts at the workbench. Carefully inspect and tune up each model as soon as it comes out of the box.

You should have handy your NMRA standards gauge, a sharp modeler's knife, a set of needle files, graphite powder lubricant, small tweezers, and a good pair of needle nose pliers. These tools and supplies will be useful for removing burrs, smoothing parting lines, lubricating moving parts, and making adjustments in general. Let's look at two major areas of concern:

● **Trucks:** Make sure the wheels are gauged properly and spaced evenly between the side frames. Figure 10 shows how to check the gauge with an NMRA gauge. You can usually slide the wheels on the axle by holding opposing wheels and twisting while pushing or pulling.

Make sure all four wheels touch the rails at the same time. I use a glass plate for this, as a piece of track could be uneven. Rigid trucks can be a bit warped and need some twisting, while sprung trucks can have a little flash restricting their movement. Make sure the truck rolls freely without wheel wobble.

In many kits the truck-mounting screws are also used to secure the floor and car weights to the frame. In my opinion these screws should be used only to mount the trucks, so I ACC all of the subassembly pieces together to make a one-piece unit. Then I can snug up or back off the screws to adjust the car's running characteristics without worrying about whether the car will fall apart. Should a car wobble, try tightening the truck screw on one truck fairly snug to maintain stability, meanwhile leaving the truck on the other end free to rock and accommodate any irregularities in the trackwork.

● **Couplers.** I recommend converting to Kadee couplers at the outset. They are the best available, but do require careful installation. Read the instructions, then be sure to remove *all* flash and parting lines with a knife or needle file.

Sometimes a little filing of the bolsters or adding a thin washer between the bolster and the trucks is necessary to adjust the coupler height.

After your cars have been painted, aged, and sealed, apply a fine dusting of graphite on the knuckles — this will allow two cars to couple together with very little pressure. This last little trick really makes coupling a breeze.

BE FUSSY!

I recommend taking every car and locomotive off the layout, returning each one only after it passes a complete inspection. You'll find a few things to fix, but your railroad will run better as a result.

Now that you've got a fleet of reliable, sharp-looking locomotives and cars, you're ready to send trains out across those wide-open spaces around Jerome and Clarkdale. Trouble is, we don't have any wide-open spaces yet! We'll add them next.

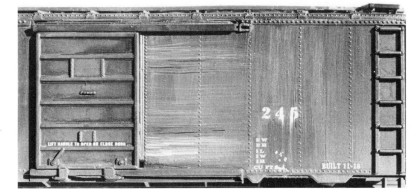

◄ Fig. 9. This touch may escape notice at first but makes cars look right. John scratched in the horizontal scars, caused by the door sliding open and shut, with an X-acto knife.

◄ Fig. 10. An NMRA standards gauge belongs in every HO modeler's toolbox. John is using it to check wheel gauge.

Backdrops for the Jerome & Southwestern

We add wide-open spaces to the railroad with personality

WHAT a difference a scenic backdrop makes! Without it our eyes rove across beautiful three-dimensional scenes only to crash into cement-block basement walls or — worse yet — wood paneling with its distracting grain. Either texture, or any other out-of-scale full-size pattern for that matter, overpowers our miniature world and ruins the effect we've worked so hard to achieve.

Now building a backdrop isn't particularly "railroady," like laying track or detailing locomotives, so many of us put it off. That's too bad, because when you consider how easy a backdrop is to build and and how little time it takes, the work put into a backdrop pays a big, big dividend. Our last strong tie with the real world is broken, and the illusion we wanted when we set out to build the railroad in the first place is reinforced and completed.

The techniques I used to build the backdrops for the Jerome & Southwestern require no artistic ability whatsoever. All you have to be able to do is paint a piece of Masonite, cut a shape out of a piece of paper, and cement that shape to the Masonite. In fact, it took me only 5 minutes to demonstrate the technique in Kalmbach's first videotape, BUILDING MODEL RAILROAD SCENERY WITH THE EXPERTS.

These backdrops will work for any layout, big or small, so whether you're building the J&S or not, I hope you'll find some thoughts here that will help you bring a little backdrop magic to your own railroad.

SOME BACKGROUND ON BACKDROPS

Because the Jerome & Southwestern is such a small and accessible railroad, we got away with putting off the backdrops until we'd finished it. If you're building a big, basement-sized railroad, you'd be smart to think about building the backdrop early on, or at least figuring out how you're going to do it when the time comes. Otherwise you can quite literally build yourself into a corner that you can't get to with anything less than one of those phone company-type cherry pickers.

Some modelers paint simple, flat, no-nonsense, solid blue backdrops; others paint elaborate landscapes. As I've said before, I'm not a believer in hard-and-fast rules, but here are some of my basic principles for effective backdrops:

● The backdrop shouldn't steal the show. It shouldn't be more detailed than the three-dimensional modeling in front of it.

● Obviously the backdrop should be in character. You don't want a desert scene behind a model of Pennsylvania's Horseshoe Curve!

● The colors shouldn't be too bright. Remember, the backdrop creates the illusion of distance. Colors seen from a distance are grayed and muted by haze.

● Avoid airplanes in flight and other subjects normally in motion. Trucks and cars

Same lighting, same railroad, same everything, but what a difference the backdrop makes! A blue sky and some paper landscape makes the 4 x 8-foot Jerome & Southwestern look like it goes on forever.

come with a sky already printed on the paper, but I recommend trimming it away and using your own sky. Then you won't have to worry about seams.

THE MASONITE PANELS

I built my 2-foot-high backdrop boards from 1/8" tempered Masonite framed and braced with pine. See fig. 1. I glued and clamped the 1 x 2s to the Masonite and allowed the glue to cure overnight. The backdrop panels screw to the edges of the layout and are easily removable; that way the artwork, time, and money aren't permanently sacrificed to a wall that must stay if I should move.

It's a good idea, incidentally, to cove inside corners like the one behind the Jerome Mining District so that the intersecting skies don't collide at a 90-degree angle. In this case, though, I used the mountain to hide the corner.

I painted my sky with ordinary latex house paint. The basic blue color you might choose is a matter of personal taste, although I recommend keeping it on the light side.

After picking out and buying my basic blue, I poured off some into a separate container and made a darker version by stirring in some ultramarine blue. I made a lighter version by mixing in white and a little pthalo blue. My coloring agents were acrylic artist's colors in tubes. You could also use universal dyes like those we used to color the scenery.

Once blended on the Masonite panels — lightest at bottom to darkest at top — these three shades of blue simulate depth and distance. To get an idea of the effect we're shooting for, just step outside and look at the

can be okay if they're parked or sitting at stop signs. Then you don't need an explanation for the frozen motion.

COMMERCIAL SYSTEMS

So much for a smattering of theory, now let's get into some practical application. Most of us can manage to paint a surface blue, but when it comes to adding mountains, buildings, trees, and other details we excuse ourselves and sneak away. Now one solution might be to hire an artist, but this approach is impractical and too expensive for most of us. Besides, we've done everything else on the layout ourselves, why not the backdrops too?

At least two commercial backdrop systems are available that can give us profes-

sional results in just about any situation. I used the Instant Horizons (formerly HO West) line from Walthers. Included are 12 different 24" x 36" scenes in full color. The instructions include some neat sketches and ideas by designer Tom Daniel. In fact, one of these sketches strongly influenced my design for the J&S.

Rail-Scenes by Detail Associates is another backdrop series. The artwork is excellent and the system is ingenious. Extra buildings and other details are included on the printed sheet, and by cementing these to the basic backdrop you can modify the scenes in many ways.

To use the Detail Associates system you must trim out the scenery and cement it to a painted sky. The Walthers backdrops

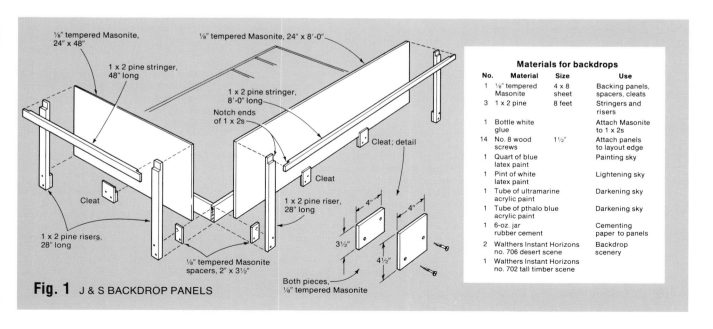

No.	Material	Size	Use
1	1/8" tempered Masonite	4 x 8 sheet	Backing panels, spacers, cleats
3	1 x 2 pine	8 feet	Stringers and risers
1	Bottle white glue		Attach Masonite to 1 x 2s
14	No. 8 wood screws	1½"	Attach panels to layout edge
1	Quart of blue latex paint		Painting sky
1	Pint of white latex paint		Lightening sky
1	Tube of ultramarine acrylic paint		Darkening sky
1	Tube of pthalo blue acrylic paint		Darkening sky
1	6-oz. jar rubber cement		Cementing paper to panels
2	Walthers Instant Horizons no. 706 desert scene		Backdrop scenery
1	Walthers Instant Horizons no. 702 tall timber scene		

Materials for backdrops

Fig. 1 J & S BACKDROP PANELS

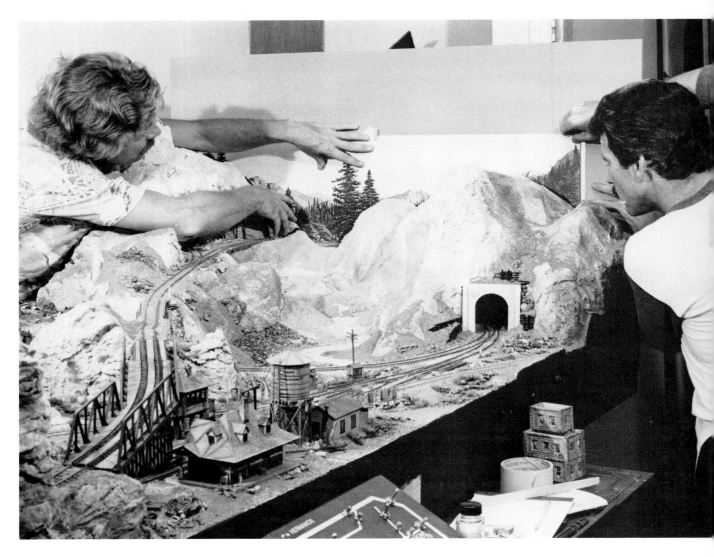

range of blue in the outdoor sky at midday.

I painted my panels with a small spray gun, making sure to thin the paint properly for spray application. You can do the job just as well, maybe better, with a 3"-wide brush. See fig. 2. Begin at the bottom with your light blue and brush from side to side in long strokes. One-third of the way up begin using the base blue, and at two-thirds up ease in the dark version. The brush is good for sky work because it will leave some horizontal streaking as you blend from one color to the next. The streaking

may not look so good while the paint is still wet, but once it dries you'll find it a desirable feature that helps simulate haze.

PAPER MOUNTAIN MAJESTIES

Once our blue skies are thoroughly dry we can mount them temporarily to the layout and start figuring out how we'll use our paper scenes. See fig. 3. It's helpful to have a buddy who can move the paper around while you stand back and decide where it will look good. Once you're satisfied with the backdrop's position, tack it lightly in place with a few pieces of masking tape. Remove the panel from the layout and place it on a work table.

Make a registration mark on the bottom of the printed backdrop and the painted panel. This mark will help you reposition the backdrop after you've trimmed away the sky.

Carefully trim the sky away, using an X-acto knife with a sharp no. 11 blade. Cut out the mountains and other landscape shapes freehand; use a straightedge when cutting out buildings.

Now you're ready to mount the paper to the Masonite. Lay the paper on the panel, using your registration marks. Place two or three pieces of masking tape along the bottom edge to make a hinge. Fold the backdrop over and liberally apply rubber cement to the area on the backing board that will be covered by the paper. Work

quickly so the cement doesn't dry before the entire area is coated; then flop the paper over onto the rubber cement. Place a sheet of clean paper over the backdrop and use your hands to gently squeegee the excess cement toward the top edge. Remove the sheet of paper immediately.

Use a piece of masking tape, sticky side out, to pick up excess dried cement from the backing board.

That's really about all there is to making J&S-style backdrops. Working carefully, you can add some extra detail. Figure 4 shows how I use black and gray chalks to add smoke coming from chimneys. I scrub the color on with tight, circular motions, making all the plumes drift in the same direction. Sometimes the wind swirls in nature, but it looks pretty unnatural if the smoke is blowing every which direction on your layout!

THE J&S GROWS

Folks say a layout is never finished, and maybe that's true. Even when everything's running smoothly and there's scenery and structures on every square foot, you can still find details to add, change, or improve. The J&S is mighty close to finished, though — close enough to get the itch to grow. In the next chapter we'll conclude the J&S story by adding an extension, the Back Alley & Wharf. Figure 4 is a sneak preview of how the BA&W will look.

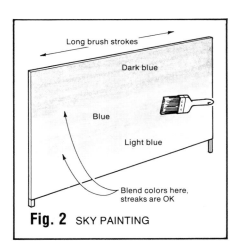

Long brush strokes

Dark blue

Blue

Light blue

Blend colors here, streaks are OK

Fig. 2 SKY PAINTING

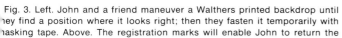

Fig. 3. Left. John and a friend maneuver a Walthers printed backdrop until they find a position where it looks right; then they fasten it temporarily with masking tape. Above. The registration marks will enable John to return the paper scene to the same position on the Masonite. He uses an X-acto knife to cut the sky away. Below: John applies rubber cement quickly and liberally to the backing panel. Once it's dried, he pulls off the excess with masking tape.

Fig. 4. John adds smoke to the backdrop with chalks and a stiff brush, first scrubbing the brush against the chalk, then against the sky. Building the bustling Back Alley & Wharf addition covered in Chapter 9.

The Jerome & Southwestern grows

We add the Back Alley & Wharf extension to the railroad with personality

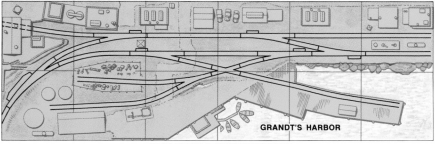

GRANDT'S HARBOR

BACK ALLEY & WHARF RAILROAD

WE'VE ALL BUT finished the Jerome &Southwestern, our Arizona-inspired 4 x 8-foot layout. Oh, sure, as they say, a layout's never finished; there's always more you can do, and I agree — you can always change the scenery here and there and work on rolling stock or structures. Still, the J&S has reached the point where most model railroaders do one of two things: they start over or they add on.

In this case I think adding on is the

This busy dock sets the theme for the 2 x 6-foot Back Alley & Wharf extension. The wharf may look like a tedious and difficult scratchbuilding project, but author Olson's methods make it go quickly and easily.

John made an effective transition from the level ground of his urban scene to the mountains of the Jerome & Southwestern by placing the buildings on the left side of the extension up on terraces. Notice that trains going behind Superior Hardware slip easily out of sight as they enter the J&S.

better decision. Instead of returning to zero train-running and operating possibilities, we've doubled our operating potential while adding less than half as much layout area.

As you look at the color photos, it should become rather obvious that when I expanded I didn't carry on with the desert theme. I wanted an addition that would look at home alongside the J&S, but at the same time I wanted to try new things. As long as I was willing to risk a thematic departure why not make it a big one? Why not abandon the desert's wide open spaces and build a crowded city waterfront?

DESIGN CRITERIA

These are the features I decided to stress in planning the new addition:

• The benchwork would be stout so I could transport the layout safely to conventions.

• The track plan would include interchange and operating potential.

• Vertical lines would be emphasized in the structures and details, so as to contrast with the horizontal lines more dominant on the Jerome & Southwestern.

• To create a crowded urban look I would use every square inch of space available.

• The buildings would house multiple occupants, so as to emphasize crowding and provide more destinations for car setouts.

• The colors would be dark, cool, and foreboding, as in most heavy industry areas.

• Clutter and junk would abound.

• I would use printed artwork on the backdrop that further emphasized the foreground theme — busy, busy, and busy.

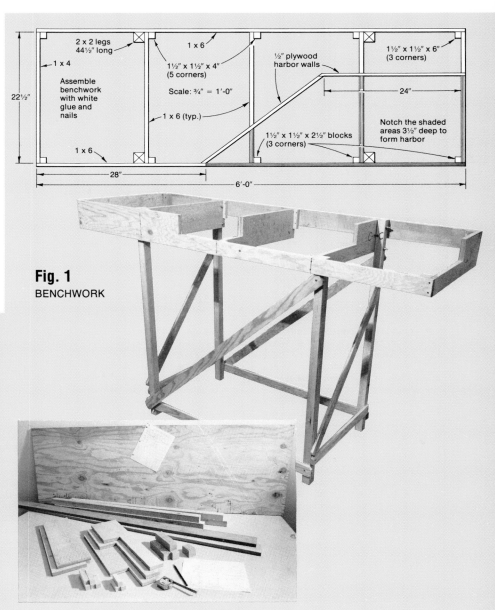

Fig. 1
BENCHWORK

Materials for benchwork

No.	Material	Size	Use
1	½" plywood	2 x 6 feet	Top
2	½" plywood	3½" x 24"	Harbor walls
2	½" plywood	2" x 22½"	Horizontal leg braces, end*
2	½" plywood	2" x 36"	Horizontal leg braces, side*
2	½" plywood	2" x 41"	Diagonal leg braces, end*
2	½" plywood	2" x 53"	Diagonal leg braces, side*
1	½" Homasote	2 x 6 feet	Roadbed
1	1 x 6 pine	6 feet	Front stringer
5	1 x 6 pine	22½"	Laterals
1	1 x 4 pine	6 feet	Rear stringer
3	1½" x 1½"	2½" pine	Corner blocks (harbor)
5	1½" x 1½" pine	4"	Corner blocks (rear)
3	1½" x 1½" pine	6"	Corner blocks
4	2 x 2 fir	44½"	Legs
2	2" C-clamps		
2	½"-dia. x 2" dowel		
7	⅜"-dia. x 3" bolts with washers and nuts		
1	½ pint white glue		
1	lb. no. 8 box nails		
24	1"-long no. 8 flathead screws		

*1 x 2 pine could also be used for bracing.

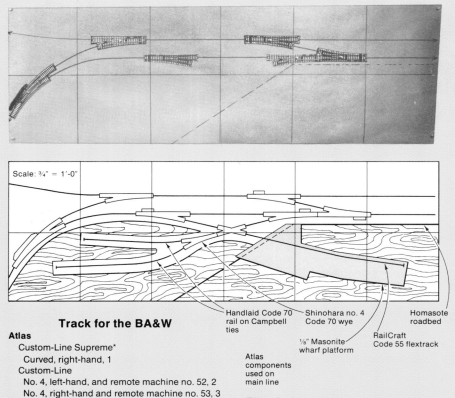

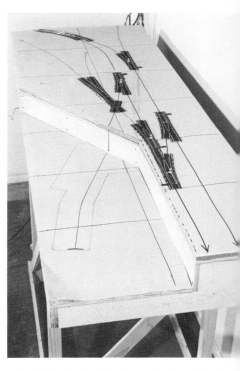

← Fig. 3. Here's the full-size track plan laid out on the finished benchwork. Later John carved away the Homasote in many areas so as to create natural rolls and depressions in the ground.

Scale: ¾" = 1'-0"

Handlaid Code 70 rail on Campbell ties — Shinohara no. 4 Code 70 wye — Homasote roadbed

⅛" Masonite wharf platform — RailCraft Code 55 flextrack

Atlas components used on main line

Fig. 2 TRACK PLAN

Track for the BA&W

Atlas
Custom-Line Supreme*
  Curved, right-hand, 1
Custom-Line
  No. 4, left-hand, and remote machine no. 52, 2
  No. 4, right-hand and remote machine no. 53, 3
  No. 123, 30 degree crossing
  Curvable track, 5
  Insulated rail joiners, 1 pkg.
  Metal rail joiners, 1 pkg.
  Track nails, 1 pkg.
Campbell
  Ties, low profile, 150
Rail Craft
  Code 70 preweathered rail, 3-foot lengths, 2
  Code 55 flexible track, 1 length
  Spikes, 100
Shinohara
  No. 4 Code 70 wye turnout, 1
*Custom-Line Supreme curved turnouts are out of production and difficult to locate. Curved turnouts by Tyco or Shinohara can be easily substituted.

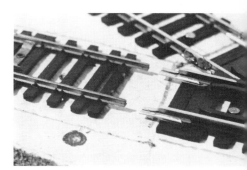

← Fig. 4. To make the transition from Code 100 rail to smaller sizes, John slid a rail joiner onto the larger rail, crimped the end flat, and then soldered the smaller rail to the flattened half.

• Locomotives and cars found most frequently on the Back Alley & Wharf would be weathered and aged to be more dingy, dirty, and dark than their bleached and dusty counterparts seen most frequently on the J&S.

Shifting my mental gears from the hot, arid, and vast Jerome motif over to the above-listed features was made much easier by spending a few hours in the industrial, railroad-laden sections of East Los Angeles. I shot a couple rolls of film to help remind me later of those buildings and details I wanted to use on the BA&W. I heartily endorse on-the-spot research like this. It provides you with an awareness and a record of all those little details that do so much to enliven the scene.

BENCHWORK

Figure 1 shows the details for making the BA&W's benchwork. I made mine entirely from plywood because I had some on hand. Using pine lumber like that recommended in the bill of materials will save a lot of cutting and make the job easier.

I used wooden pegs to give me good alignment between the BA&W and the J&S. To locate the holes for the pegs I clamped the two benchwork units together, then drilled ½" holes, holding the drill as perpendicular to the surface as I could. After separating the two units, I glued the wooden dowels into the J&S benchwork, then chamfered the peg ends to ease insertion.

TRACKLAYING

As I'd done in building the J&S, I made a full-size track plan on brown Kraft paper, using photocopies of turnouts to establish the final arrangement. Thumbtacking the paper to the wall, as shown in fig. 2, made it easy to work on.

Figure 3 shows the paper plan in place on the finished benchwork. I used Homasote for the roadbed, as I'd done on the J&S. As indicated in fig. 2, I laid the Atlas switches and Code 100 flexible track for the main line. My basic tracklaying techniques are covered in Chapter 3.

Not all the rail used on the BA&W was the same height. My technique for making the transition from one rail size to another is shown in fig. 4.

Figure 5 shows how I installed a Labelle Industries ground throw to control the Shinohara Code 70 wye turnout. The idea here was to involve operators more intimately in the train movements. I shimmed up the ground throw to the proper level on a block of pine that I later painted to look like a concrete pad.

A piece of .020″-diameter piano wire connects the ground throw to the throw rod on the turnout. I bent this wire to a Z shape so the spring action would hold the points snug against the stock rails.

← Fig. 5. Most turnouts on the J&S and BA&W are powered by electric switch machines. For the Code 70 wye John installed a Labelle Industries hand throw that would involve the operator a bit more intimately in switching operations.

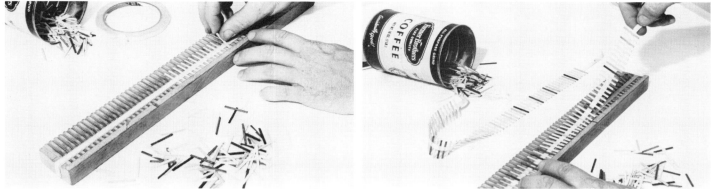

Fig. 6. Left: John makes strips of wooden ties for handlaid track in this homemade jig. Right: Masking tape holds the ties in alignment, ready to be glued to the roadbed.

Fig. 7. Top to bottom: John paints glue on the roadbed, then lays the tie strips. He uses a square to hold the ties in position while pulling the masking tape away. After the glue has dried, he sands the tops of the ties flush so there'll be no dips in the rails.

MAKING TIE STRIPS

For the paired industrial sidings on the left side of the BA&W, I went a little wild and handlaid some track, using Code 70 rail on Campbell low-profile ties. You could glue the ties one at a time directly to the roadbed, but I prefer to speed up the job by using tie strips made in a homemade piano jig.

The jig, shown in fig. 6, is made by gluing pieces of ⅛"-square stripwood to a 2-foot length of 1 x 2. The space between the ⅛"-square sticks should be 1½ tie widths. I sawed a ⅜"-wide slot through the ⅛"-square sticks for the entire length ¼" in from the side rail. This slot allows me to lay ¼"-wide masking tape in the jig sticky-side-up.

To make a tie strip I place ties in the slots, press them against the tape, then pull out the 2-foot-long finished strip.

You don't have to be a mental giant to make tie strips, and I usually knock them out 10 to 20 at a time while watching TV. I store them for later use by hanging them along the edge of the layout.

LAYING TIES

Figure 7 shows laying the ties on the BA&W spurs. Starting at the wye turnout, I painted the centerline of one siding with full-strength white glue, trying to keep it uniform and not doing more than 2 feet — more than that and the glue would probably skin over before there was time to press the ties into it.

Next I laid a strip of ties over the centerline, tape side up. I sighted down the ties from both ends and above. Once I was satisfied with their alignment, I pressed them down firmly into the glue.

A combination square makes a good tool for holding the ties against the roadbed while pulling off the tape. You could allow the glue to dry overnight and then simply pull off the tape, but I prefer to do it right away so the tape won't tend to straighten out curves. Move the square or other holding device along the ties leap-frog fashion as you work the tape off.

After the glue had completely set, I sanded the tie tops flush, using 200 grit paper and going very easy. The ties are soft wood and cut quickly. The idea is to sand only until all the ties have a little dust around them — any more is unnecessary.

SPIKING RAIL

I used Rail Craft preweathered rail and spikes and Kemtron track gauges. In addition, I rounded up a pair of diagonal cutters, needle-nose pliers, rail joiners, a Bright Boy abrasive block, and tie stain. You should also have an NMRA standards gauge. A plastic tray is handy for keeping all these tools and materials together.

Figure 8 shows how I spiked the rail, using the needle-nose pliers. Many modelers file a shallow notch across the face of one plier jaw about ⅛" from the end to help hold the spike head while pushing it in. Drive the spikes in pairs in the same tie on opposite sides of the rail. When spiking a curve, begin with the inside rail.

As you spike the second rail use the Kemtron gauges to hold it in alignment with the first. Continue spiking on down the siding, leap-frogging the track gauges one over the other. Push the spikes home until they're snug; don't press them down too hard or you'll kink the rail. I spike every four or five ties and try not to use the same tie for both rails, preferring a more random look. Once finished, I check the work carefully with the NMRA standards gauge and make necessary adjustments.

There's no law saying all of your handlaid track must be perfect. On especially derelict sidings I will omit every fifth or sixth tie, break off the ends of some, lay a few at skewed angles, and gently kink the rails up and down and from side to side. Watch the cars rock to and fro over this trackage!

Any intentional rail kinks should be severe enough to be obvious to the viewer, yet they shouldn't hinder train operations. On scenic and nonoperational foreground track I will misalign rail ends, remove prototypically long 39-foot rail sections, and raise general havoc with my scale section crews.

Once all the rail was spiked firmly in place, I washed a dilute mixture of tie stain over the completed track, scrubbing my way along and making some ties darker than others, as shown in fig. 9.

WIRING

I wired the BA&W addition using the same basic two-cab, common-wire system I explained back in Chapter 3. Figure 10 indicates the block locations, feeder attachment points, control panel details, and materials needed. With this system you can control any electrical block from either of your two power packs by throwing the single-pole, double-throw electrical switch governing that block in the direction of the power pack.

Only the wye tracks require any special wiring. If you've built the J&S and now are adding the BA&W, the wye junction between the two will function electrically as a reverse loop. Refer to installment 3 for information on how to wire it.

Because I used a pin-type connector to continue the wiring from the J&S to the BA&W, I can disconnect quickly when I want to pull the BA&W out and take it to a show or convention.

PLACING THE STRUCTURES

Figure 11 identifies the structures I used on the BA&W. One reason the urban addition doesn't clash with the desert layout is that these buildings were kept small and unassuming. Notice that some of the buildings are placed on terraces. Those amount to manmade changes in elevation that contrast with the natural, rolling topography of the J&S. Retaining walls like those shown in fig. 12 allow more acreage to be used for productive purposes, space being at a premium as it is in any busy urban area.

I laid out the urban scene on the BA&W by trial-and-error, first putting together about twice as many structures as I could actually use so I'd have plenty to choose

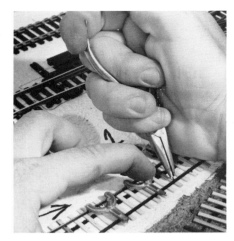

◆ Fig. 8. John uses Kemtron gauges to hold the rail firmly in gauge while he's hand spiking it.

◆ Fig. 9. The last step in handlaying track is brushing on stain, randomly varying the tones.

from. I didn't finish all these buildings completely, though, as I didn't want to put too much time into those that would be set aside for other projects.

As fig. 13 shows, once I'd made up my mind, I marked each building and its location. This allowed me to add final details, paint, and signs at the workbench where working conditions were more convenient.

ROADS, SIGNS, FENCES, AND DIRT

Once I knew where the buildings would

go, I sketched on the route for the concrete roadway, as shown in fig. 14. Note in these photos that many details have been temporarily placed on the layout to check how they might fit. As the photos of the finished layout show, some of these ideas were kept; others silently slipped away.

Industrial areas like this abound with signs and billboards. I made model versions from stripwood, Plastruct structural shapes, and cardstock. I used printed signs from Chooch and Fine Scale Miniatures, as

Structures

Key	Manufacturer and item	Kit No.	Key	Manufacturer and item	Kit No.
1	AHM repair shop	5815	11	Atlas signal tower	704
2	Yorke tanks, 2 small, 1 large		12	Atlas Burns Engineering Corp.	747
3	MDC telegraph office	1506	13	Campbell warehouse	373
4	Port Plastics, scratchbuilt		14	Used car lot, scratchbuilt	
5	Atlas lumberyard	750	15	Warehouse, scratchbuilt	
6	Kibri cement hoppers	9952	16	Atlas Burns Engineering Corp.	747
7	Junkyard, scratchbuilt		17	Model Dynamics freight house	30302
8	AHM Uncle Joe's Barber Shop	5738	18	Magnuson Gemini Building	802
9	Chooch loading dock	9005	19	Stewart diesel facilities	103
10	Cider works, Plastruct shapes		20	Magnuson Bill's Glass Shop	803

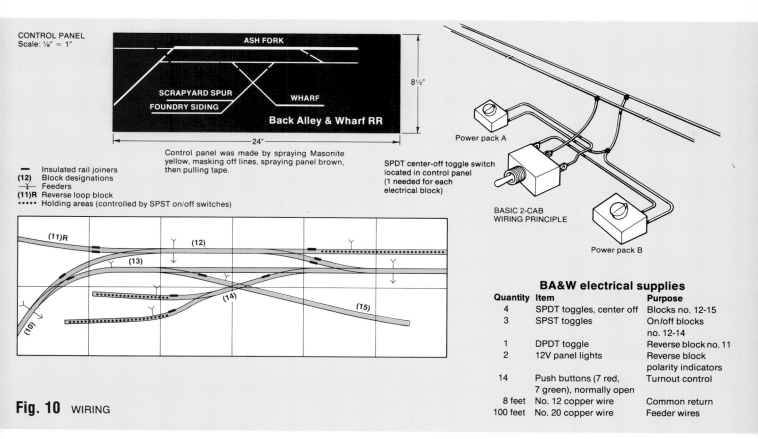

CONTROL PANEL
Scale: ⅛″ = 1″

ASH FORK

SCRAPYARD SPUR   WHARF

FOUNDRY SIDING

Back Alley & Wharf RR

8½″

24″

Control panel was made by spraying Masonite yellow, masking off lines, spraying panel brown, then pulling tape.

SPDT center-off toggle switch located in control panel (1 needed for each electrical block)

Power pack A

BASIC 2-CAB WIRING PRINCIPLE

Power pack B

— Insulated rail joiners
(12) Block designations
⊤ Feeders
(11)R Reverse loop block
•••• Holding areas (controlled by SPST on/off switches)

(11)R
(12)
(13)
(14)
(15)
(10)

Fig. 10 WIRING

BA&W electrical supplies

Quantity	Item	Purpose
4	SPDT toggles, center off	Blocks no. 12-15
3	SPST toggles	On/off blocks no. 12-14
1	DPDT toggle	Reverse block no. 11
2	12V panel lights	Reverse block polarity indicators
14	Push buttons (7 red, 7 green), normally open	Turnout control
8 feet	No. 12 copper wire	Common return
100 feet	No. 20 copper wire	Feeder wires

Fig. 11
STRUCTURES

17   18   19   20

The backdrop and buildings against it create an illusion of distance, even though the scene here is only about 18″ deep. Mini-scenes, like the automobile in difficulty at lower right, add much character to the model railroad.

▲ Fig. 12. To make a terrace John glued rock wall castings to the front of a Styrofoam block.

▲ Fig. 13. Once he decided where a building would go, John marked both the building's location and the building itself with a marking pen.

▲ Fig. 14. Left to right: To make his concrete road, John first roughed in the outline on the layout itself. Then he pinned strips of tracing paper to the layout and taped them together with masking tape to make a pattern. After transferring the pattern to heavy, gray illustration board, he cut the road out. He glued the road to the layout, then used a black, fine-point pen to draw cracks and joints as well as outline tar-patched areas. He used Magic Markers in two different tones of gray to represent both fresh and old asphalt patches. John finished by dusting black chalk along the center of each lane where oil and grease would naturally tend to accumulate.

well as some I cut from old issues of MODEL RAILROADER. Dry transfer lettering came in handy for some signs, and I also used Micro Scale billboard and sign decals. You can hardly have too many signs in an industrial area like this — I stopped counting after I'd made a hundred!

Variety is the key when it comes to fences. I made all kinds: chain link, box-wire, corrugated steel, and wood. Figure 15 shows my method for making chain-link fences. Fences are usually the victims of heavy postering, so here's a place where you can use dozens of more signs!

As I'd done on the J&S, I covered the ground with real dirt, bonding it with diluted white glue from a spray bottle. Because this is a dingy industrial area I used dark colors. Also, I used thin spray solutions of umbers and blacks to stain the earth.

I used ballast only on the main line. Ties on the sidings were buried, or nearly buried, in the earth.

THE SEAWALL

A distinctive waterfront feature is the rip-rap seawall. As fig. 16 shows I made it easily by gluing crushed granite from a local masonry supply house onto a triangular block of Styrofoam. Don't do as I did and forget to paint the top surface of the foam a dark color before gluing on the rocks. Later I added drain pipes, a culvert, and a fence along the top edge.

I made the sewage flowing from the various drain pipes by soaking strands of cotton in polyester resin and quickly stuffing one end into the pipe while allowing the other end to rest on the water surface. I also added a plaster rock casting to break the monotony of a long seawall.

BUILDING THE WHARF

The pier and its surroundings are the real theme setter. Figure 17 shows the steps I took in building it.

I started by cutting a piece of 1/8"-thick, tempered Masonite to use as the main platform. Next I drilled 1/8"-diameter holes in a pattern like those I'd seen on many real-world wharves. I cut 4"-long piles from 1/8" wood dowels and glued them into the holes. I test-fitted this assembly to the railroad. Once I was happy with it, I overlapped it by 1" onto the Homasote roadbed and epoxied it in place. Then I glued a few taller pilings to the edge of the deck.

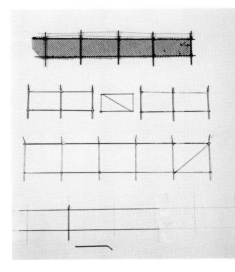

▲ Fig. 15. Bottom to top: To make a chain-link fence, John first draws a pattern on cardboard. He then tapes on brass rod horizontal members, tapes the uprights in position, and solders the frame. The netting comes from a fabric shop. Thread along the top represents barbed wire; a little silver or gray paint completes the fence.

▲ Fig. 16. Making the seawall was a simple matter of cementing stones to a Styrofoam form.

To bond all the pilings in place I mixed up 10 ounces of polyester resin and poured it onto the plywood water surface. This bonded the 200 or so pilings firmly to the plywood, forming a water surface at the same time. Because I used twice as much catalyst as the manufacturer recommends, the surface rippled automatically.

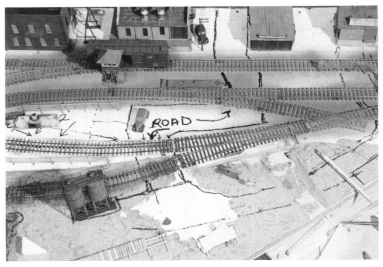

Fig. 17. Above: The wharf platform is a piece of Masonite drilled to accept ⅛"-diameter dowel pilings. Below left: After pouring resin water and painting it, John used a mixture of paint and ballast to add barnacles to the pilings. A glossy coat of liquid plastic gave the water a wet look.

MODELING THE WATER

After the resin had cured for 2 days I painted the surface with a dark green latex. Any green-black color would have done just fine. Avoid blue — it would look artificial.

After another day of curing, I mixed some raw umber, yellow ochre, and black with small containers of my basic green and splotched these mixtures randomly on the green surface. I sprayed water over the fresh paint and swirled it around with a no. 4 brush, thus creating a brackish, backwater look. You don't want the colors to mix too evenly or you'll lose that lovely oil-slicked, chemically polluted, stagnant water look. Once I was happy with the painted water, I glued junk such as tires, driftwood, and an old automobile body along the shoreline.

By now I'd worked myself into a really nautical mood. I added barnacles to the bottom ¾" of each piling by brushing on a mixture of white glue and gray ballast.

Junkyards are always interesting. Besides, they're easy to incorporate into urban scenes because they can fit a space of any size or shape. It's just about impossible to add too much detail to a scene like this.

Fig. 18
BACKDROP

Backdrop materials*

No.	Material	Size	Use
1	⅛" tempered Masonite	2 x 8 feet	Backing panel, spacers, cleats
1	1 x 2 pine	6 feet	Stringer
2	1 x 2 pine	28"	Risers
1	Detail Associates no. 7501 backdrop		City scene
1	Detail Associates no. 7503 backdrop		Industrial scene
1	Walthers no. 711 backdrop		Freight yard scene

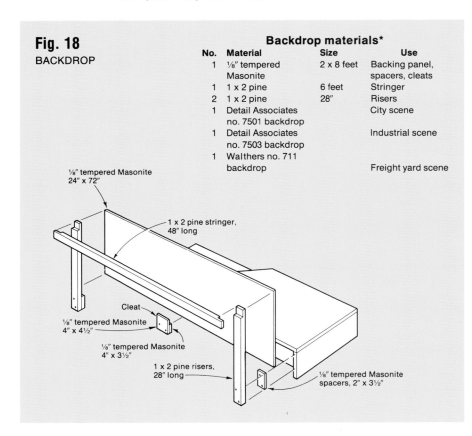

⅛" tempered Masonite 24" x 72"

1 x 2 pine stringer, 48" long

Cleat

⅛" tempered Masonite 4" x 4½"

⅛" tempered Masonite 4" x 3½"

1 x 2 pine risers, 28" long

⅛" tempered Masonite spacers, 2" x 3½"

To finish the water I brushed on Varathane brand finishing plastic, using a scrubbing motion to create swirls around the pilings.

I epoxied Rail Craft's Code 55 flextrack to the Masonite deck. This simulates the light rail usually found in such situations. I found the Code 55 rail very easy to bend, but also easy to kink. You must be careful when handling it, but it looks super and really contrasts with the Code 100 rail used on the main line.

To finish off the deck I glued sections of 1/16"-thick, ⅛"-scribed siding to the Masonite and butted it against the ends of the ties to simulate planking. I glued .020" x .125" stripwood planks between and along the rails.

THE BACKDROP

Figure 18 shows the materials and methods I used to make the backdrop. The techniques were the same as those I explained in Chapter 8. Using an X-acto knife I cut the buildings from commercial paper backdrops; then I rubber-cemented them to a blue-painted Masonite panel.

The backdrops by both Walthers and Detail Associates are excellent products. By cutting away the sky portions of all three, I was able to combine and recombine the elements into a custom backdrop designed especially to fit the BA&W. Rail Scene backdrops even include extra signs, buildings, and vehicles in the sky area.

Fig. 19. The Back Alley & Wharf was not planned so much as it just grew. The final design was arrived at by constantly trying new arrangements of structures, details, and backdrop buildings.

BA&W fans must be night owls. Like so many railroads operating in busy urban areas, the BA&W likes to work in the wee hours when there's less automobile and truck activity to hold up the action.

Making a backdrop that matches the three-dimensional modeling is largely a matter of trial-and-error. Although I'm describing it toward the end of the story, we actually designed the backdrop gradually as we went along. Figure 19 shows my friend, Ed Johnson, who has an excellent eye for such things, adjusting the models, backdrops, fences, and roads as he works out the elements of a scene. Once happy with a scene we would let it sit for a few days and check it again with fresh enthusiasm. Sometimes we'd see things we missed during the initial session.

I finished the backdrop by airbrushing on smoke, smog, and haze to enhance the industrial look. The sky on the left side needed to match the J&S, but as I worked toward the right, I made the sky darker. As the smoke patterns show, there's a prevailing wind from left to right to help legitimize the cleaner air at the left side.

CONCLUSION

The color photos are your best source of information about all the final details. I added lights inside buildings and also some to light up outdoor activities. Lots of miniscenes feature people working together. There are tractor-trailers, boats, ladders, and all sorts of waterfront details.

The BA&W is a good place to try special effects and experimental techniques. Tom Daniel once told me of an idea he had to model an industrial area as it would look just after a rainstorm. Roofs on rolling stock would be wet, puddles of water would appear between the tracks, buildings would be water-streaked, and paved areas would be shiny.

You could investigate scenic lighting, adding items like chase lights on marquees. You could make neon lights by painting Plexiglas flat black, then scratching lettering into the paint. When a bulb is placed behind, the light will show through the scratches only. Such signs would look great at back doors to bars!

Other lighting possibilities are randomly lighted windows in multistory buildings, flickering lights in industrial buildings to represent welding, and headlights in autos via fiber optics.

Then there's sound. You could add fog horns, buoy bells, truck horns, voices, and the clatter of machinery.

Animation possibilities are good here too. You could have crossing gates, oil pumps, conveyors between buildings, working machinery inside buildings, a street car moving back and forth to be viewed peek-a-boo fashion between buildings, and much more. Look around any industrial area and you'll find all sorts of ideas for features you can use on your pike.

ADIOS FOR NOW

We've come to the end of our story. If you already have a model railroad, I hope you found some useful ideas along the way. For you other guys, I hope the saga of the Jerome & Southwestern has inspired you to take the plunge and build that first small railroad. Who knows, now that you've got the idea, maybe you'll add a third section, then a fourth, and your version of the J&S will keep right on growing.

Its work done for the day, J&S switcher 07 idles quietly beside the diesel servicing facility at Ash Fork. Most industries on the BA&W extension are named for author Olson's friends and fellow model railroaders, including many who helped with the layout.

A last look at the Jerome & Southwestern

Thanks to all the personalities who helped build the railroad with personality

LIVING WITH THE J&S as it came into being, then watching the story unfold in the pages of MODEL RAILROADER magazine, has been a lot of fun for me — and for others. Although the J&S is a railroad that one person can build and enjoy, I had a lot of help, both physical and spiritual. In fact, good friends stepped in and saved me from myself at many, many points along the way.

THE PEOPLE WHO HELPED

Thanks go first to Ron Dickson, who, in addition to lending third and fourth hands when my two would not suffice, contributed suggestions, constructive criticism, much-needed counsel, and a place to build the layout. The J&S was six months abuilding in the back room of Ron's design studio, which may never be quite the same.

Carl Fallberg (also known as Fiddletown and Copperopolis Ray) created the neat J&S herald as only Carl could.

Malcolm Furlow invested that most valuable of commodities, time, in the J&S. He

Above: There's plenty of activity on the Ash Fork waterfront, even after dark. This crowd is probably up to no good — one of the rowboats is already sinking. Below: The Back Alley & Wharf's tightly packed urban clutter was inspired by prototype industrial trackage like this, in East Los Angeles.

planted, one at a time, thousands of bunch grass weeds on the hillsides and in the gullies around Cleopatra Hill and Clarkdale. Malcolm also built the mine that provides most of the railroad's traffic.

Walt Green reviewed the text and helped me make sure it all made sense. Walt has a special place at the river bottom just below Dos Hermanos depot.

Ed Johnson helped me keep going long enough to finish the BA&W extension. The arrangements of the structures and cityscape background there are principally his creative work.

Photographer Gary Krueger rushed in with his 4 x 5 view camera, set up, exposed his film, and departed just as quickly. The results were the beautiful "family room" photos on pages 3 and 10.

Michael Lloyd waved his arm (and his airbrush) at cloudless skies and brought new horizons to the J&S.

My daughter Heidi helped throughout the project, especially with the scenery and in serving as a model when I had to be behind the camera. Whether it was collecting gravel and weeds in the desert, mixing plaster, or just being there, she was a partner I could count on.

John E. McMillan shared several hours of his busy day with me, painting a verbal picture of Jerome in its heyday. His first-

hand account was a treasure I could have come by no other way.

The J&S was enriched through the eyes of Harper Goff, and his visits enlightened all present as well.

Special thanks go to my grandfather, Alfred Olson, who, as freight agent for the Great Northern in Minnesota, helped develop my lifelong interest in railroading.

THE ORGANIZATIONS

Organizations and companies helped as well. The Jerome Historical Society is to be commended for its work and for the help it provides to interested visitors like me.

Dick Appel and Clarence Menteer of Roundhouse Products helped with advice, and Dick's catalog sketches helped spark ideas for the J&S.

Hobby shops are the lifeblood of model railroading, and my thanks go to four of them for helping me find the things I needed to build the J&S: Jan and Dan Bradley of the Little Depot in Anaheim, California; Fred Hill of the Original Whistle Stop in Pasadena, California; Betty and Thatcher Darwin of the Train Station in Burbank, California; and Sue and Dick DeWitt of DeWitt's Railroads in Winter Park, Florida.

DEDICATION

This book is dedicated to Ann and Jim Olson, my wonderful parents, who cast this free spirit onto the roadbed of life.